Great Western Railway Halts

Volume 2

ISBN 0-9542035-2-6

Published by
KRB Publications
2 Denewulf Close
BISHOPS WALTHAM
Hants
SO32 1GZ

Printed by The Amadeus Press.

Front cover:

57xx No. 5744 passing Mount Hawke Halt with an up freight in July 1961. P.W. Gray / Colour Rail BRW 1521.

Great Western Railway Halts

Volume 2

by
Kevin Robertson

KRB Publications

Early days at Brimscombe Bridge Halt, @ 1903.

— Contents —

Appendices;

Early spring in the Stroud Valley, March 1953 and with No. 1406. *G.F. Heiron*

Introduction, Acknowledgements and Sources

In presenting the second and concluding part of GREAT WESTERN HALTS, I am first of all conscious of the considerable time-scale that has elapsed between the first volume and now long out of print, and this work. Suffice to say that the manuscript has lain complete but untouched for several years now, although a side benefit of this has been that even more information has come to light. Even so there has to be a cut-off date at some time and accordingly what is recorded is correct - to the best of my belief, to that available by the end of Summer 2002. What is perhaps even more surprising is that despite referring to some locations that closed almost a century ago, new information is still occasionally being uncovered.

I am delighted also to record my thanks to those individuals who have taken the time and trouble to write as a result of the publication of the first volume, - a list of these is appended at the end of this section.

In consequence of the various new pieces information it has also been possible to unravel a little more of the mysteries surrounding the 'Halt' and 'Platform' topic - far more so than the simple provision of a few sleepers and a nameboard!

As before the main body of the book is devoted to the halts and stopping places themselves and lettered 'M' to 'Y', not surprisingly minus the letter 'X'. Neither can I find any reference to a location named 'Z..... Halt' - unless of course you know different!

Similarly as in Volume 1, I have made a deliberate choice to leave out from the main text closure dates that occurred after 1948. To do otherwise would be like reading an obituary list. However in response to several requests, a separate appendix of post Nationalisation closure dates covering both this and the previous volume has been included.

I should also state that my main source references are the obvious GWR Traffic / Engineering / and General Managers minutes, as well as the invaluable official publication, '1928 List of GWR Halts'. Other sources include the various track plan books by R.A.Cooke and the same author's 'GWR Atlas for 1947'. I have also consulted the various 'Registers of Closed Stations and Halts' by C.R. Clinker, published by Avon Anglia and the Oakwood Press book, 'Private and Untimetabled Stations'.

Individual books, mainly 'line history' type volumes have also been referred to, reference to these being made under the appropriate entry. It is though only too apparent in researching a volume such as this that on occasions an author may be in dispute with official records over certain of the information. That is not to say either is correct or incorrect, as research can sometimes reveal contradictory facts. I can only state that what is contained within these pages is as accurate as it has been possible to obtain.

Finally to the acknowledgements. Foremost amongst these must be Stehen Berry. Stephen kindly took the trouble to contact me after the first volume with much valued comment and suggestion. When I then advised him Volume 2 was under way this new information became a proverbial torrent, all of it constructive and fulfilling. He has also kindly made available a most useful summary of the various ticket arrangements encountered and which is likewise included. Thank you for all your efforts.

In addition and aside from those names already mentioned in Volume 1 who are deservedly carried forward to this volume, I must record my thanks to the following. David Abbott for support and access to his amazing collection of Paddington material, Austin Attewell - for permission to search through his amazing collection of GWR photographs, many taken with such forethought. John Dagley-Morris - for assistance with photographs, David Hyde - for friendship, support and some amazing last minute additions including the quote on the rear cover, Stan Gardiner - for assistance with photographs. Ian Pope - for hospitality and also much new information on his beloved Forest of Dean and also for permission to rummage through many boxes of photographs. Paul Strong - for friendship. Michael J. Tozer - for valued new information particularly on the Bristol area. Ralph Tutton - for the insight into GWR policy with regard to the provision of facilities at, and the development of, the 'Halt' principal as included in Chapter 1. Lawrence Waters - again for photographs, and G. Young - for updated information appertaining to Volume 1.

Last and my no means least to Howard Sprenger for reading the text and making a number of positive suggestions. I hope the wait has been worthwhile.

Kevin Robertson.

Just to show the halt was not always the province of the railmotor and auto train, 7005 Sir Edward Elgar, passing Combe Halt on the 1035 (Sun) Herefod-Paddington service, 30 June 1963.

1

The Development of the Rail Motor Services and GWR Policy on Halts and Platforms.

Following on from the outline given in Volume 1, new information has come to light about the costs of the railmotors as originally provided. This is first mentioned in a hand-written letter, dated 11 May 1903, from the Accountants Office at Paddington to Mr. H. J. Bidder at Swindon, in which it states that the GWR Board has approved the construction of two 'Steam Motor Cars' at an estimated cost of £2,500 each. The Lot Number, 1037, is also referred to.

Evidently GWR Board approval had itself followed on from a discussion with the Traffic Committee, this latter body having met on 29 April 1903 at which the following entry is recorded:

"Read report by the General Manager stating that attention had for some time past been directed to various sections of the line where a passenger service by means of Motor Cars might be worked economically and advantageously and that, among other sections, the Stroud Valley offers an attractive field for experiments of this nature.

"It is accordingly suggested that a service might be adopted between Chalford and Stonehouse stations where there is already a considerable local traffic, a great part of which is conveyed by Omnibuses and other road vehicles and where it is now sought to establish a Tramway service which would be competitive to the Railway.

"It is suggested that as a commencement, an hourly service should be tried which could, if necessary, be increased to a half-hourly service, viz; that the single fares should be the same as those now charged by the Omnibuses, cheap return tickets could likewise be introduced.

"Facilities should also be provided for passengers to join and leave the cars at intermediate points, it not being anticipated that there will be any difficulty in complying with any requirements the Board of Trade may impose in regard to Motors stopping at selected places between Stations.

"The Locomotive Engineer has designed a Steam Motor Car capable of developing a speed of 30 miles an hour fully loaded and affording seating room for 52 passengers and it is recommended that two cars should be constructed forthwith, at an estimated cost of £2,500 each. Stabling for the cars can be provided at Chalford at a cost of £1,000 and the cost of the necessary permanent way work at auxiliary stopping places, signal work, siding connections is estimated at a further £1,000.

"The Committee approved the various proposals and agreed to recommend them to the Board for adoption."

As was documented previously, the Stroud Valley service did indeed commence as anticipated and with satisfactory results. So much so that as early as 2 December 1903 the Traffic Committee sent a proposal to the Board for the establishment of similar services between:

Southall and Brentford
Yealmpton, Plympton and Saltash
Teignmouth and Paignton
Worcester (Shrub Hill) and Malvern Wells.

It was thought that 12 additional cars, but of lighter build, would be required, this time at an estimated cost of £21,000.

Shortly afterwards, on 20 January 1904, a slight modification to the technical requirements of the new vehicles was made when it was announced that these should also be capable of carrying, '... heavy luggage, mails, market produce and also of hauling carriage trucks, horse boxes and trunks of goods'. Then on 19 February comes the first mention of trailer cars, albeit only two at this time, but with no cost quoted.

Meanwhile approval was also given for the necessary infrastructure at the various locations where the service was to be introduced and which included on 11 May 1904 the erection of a corrugated iron shed at Southall. The cost of this was put at £660. Was this then an early thought to servicing the cars within a separate environment?

At Paddington however, the Accountants Office had picked up the comment about the two trailer vehicles referred to earlier and added in a letter to Swindon, ".....am unable to trace any minute authorising their construction."

This was of course subsequently resolved, these two vehicles at first considered as part of a batch of 12 authorised earlier, six of which were to be built at Swindon and with outside contractors invited to tender for the remainder.

Later, in October of the same year, 1904, a reference is found to an authorisation for £50,000 to be spent on 30 vehicles, described as 12 for suburban traffic, 12 for branch traffic and six trailer cars 'for use when traffic is heavy.' These were respectively to Lots 1079, 1078, 1055 and 1081. Lot No. 1055 referring to the two trailers previously completed and Lot. 1081 to the remaining four. Shortly afterwards these orders were increased still further with an additional £80,450 authorised for 30 railmotors and 14 trailers each of which would be 70ft. long. (As an aside, trials were also taking place around this time with a trailer and what was destined to become auto-train working. One of these involved a 70' car tested by being propelled over the lightly-laid, and then still independent Lambourn branch from Newbury. Whilst the result, as far as the Lambourn line was concerned simply confirmed that a vehicle of this size was unsuitable for that branch as then equipped, the concept of auto-working was established and was of course used to considerable effect by the GWR and its successor BR(W) for the remainder of the life of the steam engine. Ironically despite being relaid shortly afterwards with heavier permanent way, auto working was never utilised on the Lambourn line.)

Returning to the expansion of the steam railmotor service, several outside firms were invited to tender for the new vehicles. These included Kerr Stuart for 14 vehicles and the Gloucester Carriage & Wagon Co. for eight. The Bristol Carriage & Wagon Co. were similarly invited to tender for six trailers.

By the spring then of 1908 the GWR were

therefore operating some 99 steam railmotors together with an associated number of trailer vehicles. Details of the original engine numbers are published in Part 11 of the RCTS series on GWR locomotives.

This same volume also contains an invaluable table of services worked by these vehicles, which is further supplemented by information in Parts 12 and 13. The reader is also referred to the booklet *Auto trains and Steam Railmotors of the Great Western* and published by the Great Western Society in 1981.

With the concept of suitable vehicles established the story of the Halt now moves away to the provision of the considerable number of new stopping places throughout the system and which would be served by railmotor and auto-train.

As is apparent from both Volume 1 and the present work, the facilities provided at the various stopping places also varied considerably,which in itself led to considerable difficulties for the operating departments. Indeed by 1923 discussion was taking place as to some possible radical measures for future development, although the practical aspect was perhaps not always considered...

Report of meeting on July 5 1923, of Committee appointed by Officers (Minute No. 9602) to Consider the Construction of Halt Platforms.

Present:
Mr. H.L. Wilkinson (Chairman)
Mr. H.R. Griffiths
Mr. S. Morris
Mr. F.R. Potter (co-opted as Mr. J.R. Morris on leave)
Mr. H. Warwick
Mr. F.W. Green (Secretary)

a.   Provision of Low Ballast Platforms.
Seventy-two per cent of the 234 halts at present in use are of standard height, and 12 halts are of the type known as 'low ballast'; in the latter cases the passengers entrain and detrain from the ballast by climbing up and down footboards. This is most inconvenient and undesirable, and the practice cannot be recommended for general adoption, even at places where the traffic is light.

The steps on rail motor cars and trailers for use at platforms not of standard height have not proved a success. They were frequently damaged and in any case they are inconvenient and dealing with passengers by steps is a tedious process. The L.M.&S. Co. have a better type of step, but it is not considered that any steps outside the framework of the coach are satisfactory.

The height of the platform must necessarily be governed by the type of vehicle used if the convenience of passengers is to be studied. It is recommended that where the traffic is light a special type of coach should be constructed with steps inside the coach leading down to a low vestibule 1 foot 6 inches above ballast level, and doors on both sides so that passengers can detrain without inconvenience at places where no raised platform is provided. Experience at a platform 1 foot 6 inches high showed that this gave an easy step from the footboard, whereas a 2 foot platform gave an awkward step.

The vehicle could either be attached at the rear of a train formed with ordinary stock or be worked separately. The Guard should ride in the vehicle to keep a special watch on the doors, issue and collect tickets and arrange by a bell signal for the stopping of the train, very much as the conductor does in a road bus. Doors both on the low (or

GWR Railmotor No. 11 at Stonehouse and probably soon after the service had commenced. This was also one of the early batch of vehicles having been completed at Swindon as early as June 1904 and displays the deep crimson lake livery of the period. Although affording a valuable and popular service the vehicle still required a crew of three and so economy of working was limited.

Collec. Ian Pope

Bromham & Rowde Halt near Devizes and soon after opening. The confusion as regards to designations is apparent even at this early stage as here is a halt with a standard height platform! From evidence to hand it would appear the corrugated Pagoda - or more officially the 'waiting shelters' were assembled on site from parts. The sides first being bolted together to form an open box. The roof was then built at ground level before being lifted into position by a gang of men. Presumably the latter operation needed a windless day.   *Collec. Paul Strong*

vestibule) level and platform level would be required, the latter for use at platforms of standard height.

If such a vehicle could be supplied, the 'Halt' system on branch and subsidiary lines could be extended very considerably to the advantage of the Company and the travelling public, and 'low ballast' platforms could be provided at any place where circumstances permit and there is a population of upwards of 200 to be served and where convenient access to the line can be provided, viz. at bridges and level crossings. The low platforms should be of 150 feet length and have a low facing of concrete, and be provided with a standard waiting shed (20 feet x 8 feet) and lighting. Where such halts could be introduced the Company could compete very favourably with road transport, and an appreciable additional traffic would be created. There would be no working difficulty in setting up a system of stopping at a halt where there is traffic to be picked up or set down on similar lines to a tramway with selected stopping places. If any particular stopping place was not used, there would be no difficulty and very little expense in removing the lamps and shelter elsewhere.

Where trains call, it is considered that the platforms should be of standard height.

b.   Renewal of existing Halt Platforms, particularly in regard to lengths.

The general practice throughout the system is for halts to be constructed of timber in the first place, except where in cuttings and other favourable spots the platforms can be made by tipping behind a timber facing. If a halt does not prove remunerative, or if an unsuitable site has been selected, there would be little difficulty in removing it if constructed of timber.

It should be possible to say when the time arrives to renew a

timber halt whether it is likely to be required as a permanent structure, and the Engineer can then decide whether the more economical course would be to carry out the work in timber or some more durable material.

It is somewhat difficult to lay down any standard on the subject of lengths, but it is considered that the following should be worked to:-

1.   Light traffic to be dealt with by a low ballast platform served by the special vehicle now recommended.

2.   Medium traffic: platforms to be 150 feet in length and of standard height.

3.   Heavy traffic: length of platforms to be governed by length of trains or cars calling as it is most desirable from several points of view that 'pulling up' should be avoided.

On branches or lines where there are a number of halts, the platforms should, as a general rule, be of uniform length in order to avoid having to load passengers in selected vehicles and making it necessary for drivers to stop at particular spots. It is interesting to note that on the Central Wales section, short platforms 100 feet in length are being provided to accommodate seasonal traffic, which will be served by trains. The ex-Cambrian Company had two halts 9 feet in length and five halts 40 feet, 50 feet or 60 feet in length, and the coach next to the Guard's van was labelled for the halt or halts concerned and stopped opposite the platform.

The Guard issued tickets from a roll and cancelled them by a bell punch. Bell punches and tickets similar to those used on street buses are now being supplied, and these appear to be a most convenient and satisfactory method for booking to the nearest important junction station, subject to a periodical check of the tickets issued.

4

c.   Company's Obligations where Trains call.

Neither the present nor the proposed Ministry of Transport requirements make specific reference to 'halts' or 'platforms'.

At present trains of varying lengths call at 127 places which are regarded as 'halts' or 'platforms'. Accommodation, other than the waiting sheds, is provided at 28 places, and lavatory accommodation (urinal only in a few cases) is provided at 18 places; at 34 places no shelters are provided.

The respects in which the Ministry of Transport requirements as applying to 'stations' are not met at 'halts' and 'platforms' are: -

1.   Provision of lavatory accommodation
2.   Provision of shelters
3.   Height of platforms
4.   Provision of clocks

Lavatory accommodation has been provided where there is sufficient need, and the requirement says that it should be provided 'where necessary'. Such accommodation could not be provided generally in view of a number of places where no staff is employed or only employed for a part of the day. Shelters are provided, except in 34 places on amalgamated lines.

The height of platform requirements is being amended to read that the height may be less than the minimum (which will be 2 feet 9 inches) where specially agreed.

Clocks. This requirement could not generally be carried out. It appears, therefore, that the Company may continue their present practice in regard to the provision of accommodation provided at halts.

It is considered that the name halt should be retained, but there does not appear to be any necessity to continue the restriction against trains calling at halts, provided the platforms are of sufficient length to accommodate the train, or special provision is made for dealing with passengers. The restriction has already been waived at many places, and the provision of a protecting signal at the rear of station platforms is no longer required.

d.   General.

In order to meet road transport competition it is desirable to encourage the provision of halts on branch or subsidiary lines, but in the past the cost of erecting a halt has been a great bar to development. On the Main Lines, however, the erection of halts should be kept to a minimum, as although some additional traffic may be obtained, margins for Goods and Through passenger trains may be destroyed by a car or train calling at a halt, and the net result may be a loss to the Company.

It is suggested the Chief Engineer be asked to specially consider the question of the cost of providing halts of standard height where such provision is necessary. It would appear that concrete walls filled with ballast, ashes or tipping should give a cheap form of halt.

Milk and Parcels traffic is dealt with at 54 places regarded as halts or platforms, and in considering proposals for low platforms the possibility of handling milk should be borne in mind, as it should be the policy to create or develop such traffic where it can conveniently be handled. A slide for loading milk from ballast level is in use on the Central Wales section. This has answered very satisfactorily, and its general use where circumstances desire would appear to be desirable. The slide is 7 feet long and 3 feet 5 inches wide, with iron ribs, and one man can draw a churn from the ballast to the van without difficulty.

When selecting a site for a halt of any type, it is essential that regard should be paid to the possibility of its future extension or development into a station, with siding facilities.

Interestingly the criteria separating a halt from a platform in the above document appears already to have disappeared, whist in some respects the comments also contradict themselves. Most obvious of all is the general consensus so typical of any committee - in that it fails to define any definite future policy!

As will be known to the devotee of the Great Western, most of the suggestions regarding to vehicles were not adopted, although the difficulties with platform length would persist as traffic patterns changed over the years. There were also several minor instances where incidents would occur as a direct result of the limited facilities, the following being a typical example:

Fireman's eye view from the cab of No. 4555 of the approach to Hoelgerrig Halt on the joint GW - LMS line. The intending passenger has already hailed the train although the views of the driver at having to stop and restart on what was clearly an extremely sharp curve are perhaps best left to the imagination. 3 May 1964.

P.J. Garland Collec. / Roger Carpenter

Penmere Platform on the Falmouth Branch. The locomotive may well be No. 5537, this working a number of the line's services on that day.   *Joe Moss / Roger Carpenter.*

Memorandum from Inspectors Office, Portmadog. July 14 1943.

Ref: Mr. W. Roberts injured Talwrn Bach Halt.
25 May 1943.

Mr. Roberts is all right again and is out hay-making using his arm as before. I understand he had a partial dislocation at the shoulder but I do not believe he will ever mention the matter again, and Mrs. Ellis, Gatekeper, Talwrn Bach, who sees him daily says he is averse to mention the mishap. I give you the approximate number of passengers using the Halt, based on a record for July 9th a normal day for summer season:

Train	Passengers joining	Passengers alighting
5.45 a.m. Up	14	10
7.45 a.m. Up	25	2
8.15 a.m. Down	15	20
10.25 a.m. Up	5	5
12.35 p.m. Down	12	16
1.15 p.m. Down	10	15
1.50 p.m. Down	30	5
3.40 p.m. Down	2	25
4.00 p.m. Up	35	15
5.50 p.m. Down	4	8
6.55 p.m. Down	4	30
7.40 p.m. Up	-	8

The above is a record for 12 trains dealt with at this Halt daily, as there is an R.A.F. Camp near this Halt we have an occasional special of about 150 men joining or alighting as the case may be at the Halt and the platform is quite inadequate to cope with such parties.

The length of our Coast sets are 6 coaches each during the summer period and the Halt platform berths about 1½ coach length but on Saturdays most sets are 7, 8 or 9 coaches which increases our difficulties.

Tygwyn Halt likewise needs the same lengthening and figures given for Talwrn Bach would be a fair average for Tygwyn also, as regards number of passengers dealt with, and as there is an Anti-Tank camp situated near this is also a similar source of difficulty and delay and should be lengthened the same as Llanaber and Talybont Halts.

Llandanwg halt is another source of delay owing to having been erected on the wrong side of the line and it will be an easy matter to make a platform on the opposite side of the line where the Guard could see the Driver to give him the signal, instead of as now when he has to go over the fence into the field or else give it from the off-side of the train...

A short while later the Office of the Superintendent of the Line at Paddington, passed a shortened report of the incident to the General Manager and, aside from repeating the information previously reported, also added that the existing platform lengths at Talwrn Bach Halt and Tygwyn Halts were 101ft. and 71ft. respectively and recommended that both should be extended to 200ft. Due to limited passenger numbers no increase at Llandanwg Halt was recommended for the present, and there was no reference to the suggested move of the platform to the opposite side of the running line.

In general terms and a century after the commencement of the Stroud Valley service it may be asked whether the whole concept was worthwhile? To answer this, care must be taken not to apply 21st century principals to the concept, which at the time was undoubtedly seen as a means of both developing new traffic as well as countering the increasing threat of road competition. Certainly, considerable new traffic was generated but perhaps still further advantage could have been gained with the greater use of low height platforms at far more places and served by the suggested specially designed vehicles having retractable steps.

On branch and secondary routes where traffic volume was limited, this would have presented few operational difficulties, although it is accepted the main lines were another matter, and a shuttle running between two points in between the various through trains could no doubt have been considered. Regardless of the hypothesis that now applies it cannot be ignored that the GWR Halt and Platform concept was a success. As a business, as well as a service to the community, there was no room within the GWR for sentiment, so locations that failed to pay their way were ruthlessly closed. In this way then, Paddington probably used its resources to the best of its ability, allowing for the technology of the time. Had the railways had their own efficient diesel units very early on then still more might have been achieved, but then we would perhaps never have seen that epitome of GWR services, a 48xx and auto coach serving the local community and pausing at a timber platform complete with pagoda shelter.

Above: Successor to the steam railmotor services were the auto trains and which introduction and development was concurrent with the rapid increase in the provision of halts. Here in what may well be a posed view, the photographer of the *Torquay Times* has recorded the scene as witnessed the demise of auto train working, a 14xx and modern day auto-coach although still with folding steps to afford access to a ground level stopping place.

Torquay Times and Devonshire Press.

Right: Former GWR 0-6-0PT No. 3732 on a curious working which lasted over 20 years, the 12.48 p.m. (Saturdays only) mixed train from Ketley to Much Wenlock and photographed at Green Bank Halt on the double line section through Colabrookdale between Lightmoor Junction and Buildwas.

G.F. Bannister.

8

Malswick Halt on the Ledbury to Gloucester line and viewed looking towards Newent. This was one of several locations where photographs are scant, perhaps not surprisingly as well, there was not a lot to record! The cheapness of construction followed both here and at numerous other sites is also obvious, it must have purveyed a strong tang of creosote on a hot day. Facilities such as this could be provided both quickly and cheaply and in consequence the GWR could effectively respond to potential traffic especially where development had occurred away perhaps from an existing station. They could equally be closed just as quickly if lack of demand dictated. The trouble was the railway itself could not so readily be moved and as times passed so road transport secured the upper hand in the rural area often with more frequent and better accessible services.

B.J. Ashworth

McLAREN COLLIERY PLATFORM

Situated between New Tredegar and Abertysswg on the Bassaleg Junction and Rhymney Lower line. Single low wooden platform with a large waiting shed serving the McLaren Nos. 1 and 3 Collieries. Probably opened shortly after the start of mining at McLaren No 1 Pit in 1891- it is shown in the working timetable for October 1902. Known to have been closed by 1947.

MAESMELYN COLLIERY HALT

Situated on the Port Talbot Railway between Cwmavon Halt and Efail Fach Platform. Date of opening not reported but known to have been in use by 1914. Used by miners and also referred to as Maesmelyn

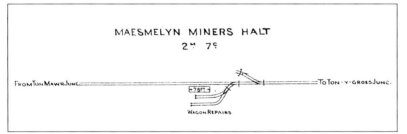

Miners Halt. Facilities comprised a simple platform 78ft in length and believed to have been devoid of any shelter. Closed sometime after 1920. The location of this stopping place was very close to the aforementioned Cwmavon Halt, and it has even been suggested that they were in fact one and the same place.

MAESMELYN MINERS HALT

see entry for Maesmelyn Colliery Halt.

MAINDY HALT

see entry for Maindy North Road Halt.

MAINDY NORTH ROAD HALT

see entry for Maindy North Road Platform.

MAINDY NORTH ROAD PLATFORM

Single platform serving the up line only north of Cathays on the Cardiff & Merthyr line. Principal use was by railmotor from Cardiff which terminated at the platform and then reversed so forming a service back to Cardiff after crossing over to the down line. Date of opening not reported although first appeared in public timetables in May 1907. Renamed Maindy North Road Halt on 10 July 1922. At a later date officially renamed Maindy Halt.

MALLWYD

Stopping place on the single line Mawddwy branch from Cemmes Road. Designated a Halt by the GWR although the suffix was not

carried. Opened in 1896, it was closed on 17 April 1901. A reference in Clinker to goods traffic having ceased on 8 April 1908 is dubious as this is not supported by the entry in the 1904 RCH Handbook. Re-opened to passengers from 31 July 1911and completely from 1 January 1931.

MALSWICK HALT

Single timber platform with wooden shelter at rear, the latter built on stilts due to the land formation. Situated on the Ledbury to Gloucester branch between Barbers Bridge and Newent. Opened 1 February 1938.

further reading: *From Ledbury to Gloucester by Rail*. Pub. Amber Graphics.

MANNINGFORD HALT

On the former Berks and Hants Extension Railway between Pewsey and Woodborough. Authorised on 17 December 1931 with up and down platforms originally of timber and footpath with steps to the nearby public road. Corrugated waiting shelters, 12ft. x 8ft., name boards, oil hut, fencing, gates and paraffin vapour lighting. Total estimated cost of £625 and opened to traffic on 20 June 1932. At a later date the

Manningford Halt	Year	Tickets issued	Season Tickets	Total Receipts £
	1932	903	8	123
	1933	1619	14	236
	1934	1514	12	179
	1935	1593	9	169
	1936	1409	14	161
	1937	1514	13	181
	1938	1238	14	168

June 1932. At a later date the platforms were replaced with concrete slabs

MARGAM HALT

Situated on the South Wales main line between Pyle and Port Talbot General, this halt was brought into use on 4 February 1948 to serve the newly opened Abbey Steel Works and consisted of two island platforms. Although unadvertised, it was served by a number of stopping trains between Swansea and Cardiff as well as having its own unadvertised workmen's trains running to and from various local stations.

MARGAN HALT

This is referred to by Cooke in *Great Western Atlas 1947*, published by Wild Swan. No other details are known. But see entry for Margam Halt.

MARINE COLLIERY HALT

see entry for Cwm Colliers Platform. The name Marine Colliery Halt was in use by 1938.

MARSTON HALT

Single platform between Titley and Pembridge and on the site of the former Marston Lane Station. Opened 26 April 1929.

MARTEG HALT

Situated on the single line between St. Harmons and Rhyader. Opened 18 May 1931, with access via steps leading down from what was later the main A479 road.

further reading: *The Mid Wales Railway*. Pub. Oakwood Press.

MARTELL BRIDGE HALT

Single platform located between Letterston and Puncheston on the North Pembrokeshire and Fishguard line. Opened 1 January 1930 and closed 25 October 1937. The location served a few isolated farms and attracted only 70 or so passengers per week.

further reading: *The Railways of Pembroke*. Pub. H.G. Waters.

MARY TAVY & BLACKDOWN HALT

Formerly a station on the Plymouth to Launceston line, it was downgraded to Halt status from 11 August 1941.

MATTHEWSTOWN HALT

see entry for Matthewstown Platform.

MATTHEWSTOWN PLATFORM

Located on the Aberdare Branch between Abercynon and Penrhiwceiber (Low Level). Opened 1 October 1914 with up and down platforms provided. Officially renamed Matthewstown Halt on 2 October 1922.

MEITHRINFA HALT

Unofficial stopping place between Aberffrwd and Rheidol Falls Halt on the narrow gauge Vale of Rheidol line. No formal facilities were provided but trains would call for the benefit of school children, many attending Miss Trotter's Meithrinfa (Nursery) School. Access from the railway was via a gateway in the railway fence.
further reading:

The Vale of Rheidol Light Railway. Pub. Wild Swan.

Marston Halt and dating from 1929. This location was one a number provided with a simpler corrugated shelter although there appeared to be little consistency in the types of shelter provided by the GWR overall and it is likely that redundant assets were re-used elsewhere.

Matthewstown Halt in its later years and displaying clear signs of neglect.

Melyncourt Halt - pre 1927 and with what may well be Railmotor No. 7 at the platform. The view illustrates well both the facilities and usage of these type of stopping places, the steeply graded pathway affording access, ballast crossing and of course the passengers.

MELYNCOURT HALT

Opened 1 June 1905 and originally provided with 200ft. long platforms opposite each other. Sometime after 1927 staggered up and down platforms were substituted. The stopping place was situated between Resolven and Clyne Halt on the Vale of Neath line.

MERCANTILE COLLIERY

Miners' stopping place believed located at the end of the branch from Tonmawr on the Port Talbot system. In use by 1899 and closed circa 1916. May also have been known as Whitworth Halt following a re-opening sometime after 1929.

MICKLETON HALT

Situated between Honeybourne and Chipping Campden. Up and down platforms 150ft. x 8ft. provided. Authorised on 27 May 1937 with footpath approaches, shelters, oil hut, paraffin vapour lighting and fencing. Estimated total cost £512. Opened on 11 November 1937 and reported as closed on 6 October 1941 although

different sources claim closure and dismantling was not until 1948.

MIDFORD HALT

Situated on the GWR single line between Limpley Stoke and Camerton and close by the crossing point of the Somerset & Dorset railway whose own Midford station was also nearby. Approval for construction was given on 24 November 1910 under the name of Midford Bridge Halt. Opened 27 February 1911 at a cost of £403. Timber construction, with standard height platform 150ft. x 10ft., corrugated pagoda shelter and access via a steeply inclined footpath from the Bath to Frome road. Closed 22 March 1915.

further reading: *The Camerton Branch*. Pub. Wild Swan

MILK PLATFORM

Single platform located between Pinged Halt and Trimsaren Road on the former BPGV system. Believed to have been used solely for milk traffic and in use by November 1938.

MILL LANE BOX

see entry for Box Mill Lane Halt

MILL STREET PLATFORM

Formerly a public platform situated at the end of the Taff Vale Railway single line from Aberdare Low Level. Authorised, at an estimated cost of £106, on 31 May 1904 and opened on 26 November 1904 consisting a single platform roughly on the site of the former

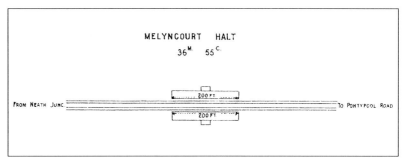

MELYNCOURT HALT

36^{M.} 55^{C.}

FROM NEATH JUNC — 200 FT — TO PONTYPOOL ROAD

200 FT

station which had been in use from 22 May 1847 to 21 November 1852. In public use until 1 June 1912 where after it was solely used by miners traffic.

further reading: *The Aberdare Railway,* Pub. Oakwood Press.

MILTON HALT

Single platform 150ft. long with pagoda shelter situated on the Banbury & Cheltenham line between Adderbury and Bloxham stations. Opened 1 January 1908. Access via a long path parallel with the single line and running to the nearest public road.

further reading: *The Banbury to Cheltenham Railway.* Pub. OPC.

MILTON HALT

original 1933 proposal. See Weston Milton Halt.

MITCHELL & NEWLYN HALT

Single 100ft. platform located on the Newquay Branch between Mount Hawke Halt and Trewerry & Trerice Halt. Opened 14 August 1905.

further reading: *The Newquay Branch.* Pub. OPC.

MITHIAN HALT

Single platform on the Truro & Newquay branch situated between Goonbell Halt and Perranporth Beach Halt. 102ft. in length and opened on 14 August 1905.

further reading: *The Newquay Branch.* Pub. OPC.

MONKS RISBOROUGH

see Monks Risborough & Whiteleaf Halt.

MONKS RISBOROUGH & WHITELEAF HALT

Situated on the joint GW/GC Aylesbury branch between Princess Risborough and Little Kimble. Single platform provided. Later renamed simply Monks Risborough. Opened 1 November 1929. Receipts included with those from Princess Risborough.

MONKTON & CAME HALT

see entry for Came Bridge Halt.

MOOR LANE HALT

Situated between Brettell Lane and Shut End on the Kingswinford

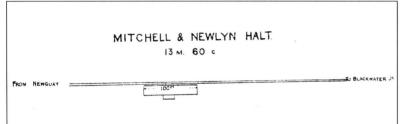

Mithian Halt in 1922 and dating from 1905. Again this is a good illustration of GWR policy in that easy access from the public road was a prime consideration when selecting possible sites.   L.G.R.P. 8842

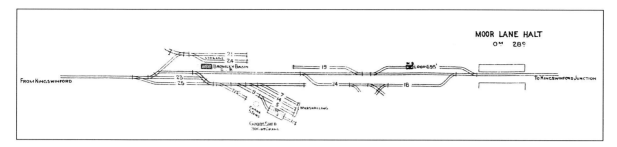

MOOR LANE HALT
0M 28C

FROM KINGSWINFORD

To Kingswinford Junction

Branch. Authorised on 15 March 1912 and at the time the aforementioned route was being widened and adapted for passenger traffic. "To be provided with up and down platforms 250ft. long with shelters and steps to the public road." It may be assumed its use as a passenger stopping place was short lived as during the period 1914-18 the location is spoken of as being used for workmen's traffic only. It is not clear if a later reversion was made to passenger working.

MOREBATH JUNCTION HALT

Authorised on 4 October 1928 with a single platform 100ft. long with alcove, fenced footpaths to road, sleeper bridge over a stream, gates and lighting. Estimated cost of £270. Opened 1 December 1928 and situated on the GWR Barnstaple branch between Morebath and Dulverton stations, close to the junction of the Tiverton and North Devon Branch. According to John Owen in his *Eve Valley Railway* book, "The halt was a quarter of a mile to the south of the village of Morebath, but there was no proper metalled road or even footpath, just a trodden track through fields. In rainy weather schoolchildren would trudge through the wet grass in boots, carrying their 'town' shoes with them. Once at the halt, the shoes would be substituted, and the boots placed tidily under the bench in the waiting shelter. The repeat performance happened in the afternoon - and the boots never went missing!"

further reading: *The Exe Valley Railway*. Pub. Kingfisher.

MOREDON HALT

Single platform 40ft. x 15ft. with checkers hut 8ft. x 9ft. situated on the former MSWJ system between Blunsden and Rushey Platt. Unadvertised, and used by workmen from 25 March 1913, possibly to 28 September 1924 and then for milk traffic only (certainly by November 1928.) Unconfirmed reports comment that other passenger traffic may have been handled. Officially closed on 1 October 1932, although receipts from the location were still being referred to in 1935. Also known as Moredon Platform.

further reading: *The Midland & South Western Junction Railway*. Pub. Wild Swan.

Transition from the old at Mitchell & Newlyn and with the modern concrete platform in sharp contrast to the oil lamp. Again there is a variation of shelter, this one affording scant protection against a Cornish gale.

L.G.R.P. 24975

Cruel perhaps, but it often seemed the smaller the stopping place the larger the nameboard! Understandable also when it is considered that the very purpose of the halt was to reach out to previously unserviced communities.

MOREDON PLATFORM

see entry for Moredon Halt

MORFA CROSSING HALT

Unadvertised stopping place situated on the Port Talbot railway between Port Talbot Docks and Margam East Junction. Up and down platforms in use by workmen from an unknown date but closed by 1933. (The name of the stopping place was taken from the dissecting Morfa Railway single line, which crossed the Port Talbot immediately at the end of the platforms.)

MORRIS COWLEY

This location is referred to by O.S. Nock in his *History of the GWR Part 3* - Pub. Ian Allan, as a Halt. It would not appear to conform with accepted Halt criteria and for information on this stopping place the reader is referred to, *The Princess Risborough - Thame - Oxford Railway*. Pub OPC.

MOSS CROSSING HALT

see entry for Moss Platform

MOSS HALT

see entry for Moss Platform

MOSS PLATFORM

Single platform situated on the Brynmally Branch north of Gwersyllt Hill Halt and opened on 1 May 1905. Reported that parcels traffic was handled. Closed 1 January 1931. Bradshaws always seemed to use the name Moss Halt and a photograph of the location taken circa 1910 shows the nameboard bearing the name Moss Crossing Halt.

MOUNT GOULD & TOTHILL HALT

Situated on the Sutton Harbour Branch at Plymouth on what was referred to as Plymouth No. 2 Loop. Up and down platforms opened on either 2 October or 2 November 1905 and closed on 1 February 1918.

MOUNT HAWKE HALT

Situated north of Chacewater on the Truro & Newquay line. Single platform 100ft. in length with corrugated pagoda shelter opened 14 August 1905.

further reading: The Newquay Branch. Pub. OPC.

Opposite page, Mount Hawke Halt in 1922 some 17 years after opening and yet with virgin chalk still apparent.

L.G.R.P. 8847

Morebath Junction Halt and proving there was always the exception to the rule in that this location was some distance from the public road. The location was also at the point of divergence of the route to Taunton and that from Tiverton, which route joined from the right. The junction Signal Box is also visible. *Mowat Collec. M309*

Moss Crossing Halt in use from 1905 to 1931 and officially designated by the GWR as a Platform. Although unconfirmed the presence of the signal box protecting the level crossing could well mean the location was staffed in that the duty included dealing with parcel and other 'smalls' traffic. *L.G.R.P. 6232*

MOUNT HAWKE HALT
1M. 51 C.

167

FROM NEWQUAY ————— 100 FT ————— TO BLACKWATER JUNC

Nantgarw Halt (High Level) on the line between Penrhos Junction and Groeswen Halt. The train is the 2.52 pm Pontypridd to Caerphilly and Machen auto-working in charge of 64xx No. 6411., on 4 September 1956.

S. Rickard

NAILBRIDGE HALT

Situated on the Forest of Dean Cinderford branch between Steam Mills Crossing Halt and Drybrook Halt. Single 150ft. platform opened on 4 November 1907 and originally not provided with any shelter. A standard corrugated pagoda was erected later. Closed on 7 July 1930.

further reading: T*he Forest of Dean Branch Vol. 2*. Pub. Wild Swan.

NANTEWLAETH COLLIERY HALT

Unadvertised stopping place on the South Wales Mineral Railway between Cymmer and Glyncorrwg. Single platform provided probably around 1940 although the colliery of the same name is known to have been in existence since 1912/16. May also have been known as Nantewlaeth Halt or Nantewlaeth Siding Halt.

NANTEWLAETH HALT

see entry for Nantewlaeth Colliery Halt

NANTEWLAETH SIDING HALT

see entry for Nantewlaeth Colliery Halt

NANTGARW

see entry for Nantgarw Halt High Level and Nantgarw Halt Low Level.

NANTGARW HALT HIGH LEVEL

Located on the former ANSW Caerphilly & Pontypridd line between Penrhos Junction and Groeswen Halt. Official records state that platforms were provided although in practice they never were. Opened 1 September 1904 and renamed from Nantgarw with effect from 1 July 1924 and to avoid confusion with the following named location. Another entry in the records refers to electric lighting to be provided at Nantgarw Halt on 14 February 1929 but it does not state which Nantgarw this was!

NANTGARW HALT LOW LEVEL

Located on the former Cardiff Railway between Glanyllyn and Upper Boat. Single platform provided and opened on 1 March 1911 and as with the previous entry the original name of Nantgawr was substituted from 1 July 1924. Parcels traffic was also dealt with.

On 7 October 1926 an entry exists in connection with the conversion of this section of the former Cardiff Railway to single line and at Nantgawr a 200ft platform on the down side with a shelter and an approach road is referred to. No cost is given. The singling was brought into effect on 16 May 1928 and with the new platform replacing what had previously been just a ground level facility. The location closed on 20 July 1931.

NANTMELYN HALT

Unadvertised stopping place situated on the Taff Vale Railway Dare Valley branch near the terminus at Bwllfa Dare. In use by miners from 1 June 1904 although for the first ten years of its existence no platform was provided. At varying intervals it was also referred to as Nantmelyn

The same location as opposite but depicted just a few years earlier in 1952 and with the structures in somewhat better condition. The 'pens' used to restrain passengers until released by the guard are apparent whilst the shelters no doubt owe their background to the originating ANSW Railway Company.
L.G.R.P. 26842

Platform. Supervised by the Aberdare Station Master and believed closed by 1948..

NANTMELYN PLATFORM

see entry for Nantmelyn Halt.

NANTWEN

Situated between Trelewis Platform and Bedlinog. Used by miners from about July 1897 and renamed Nantwen Colliery after November 1915. Ceased to be used after 1928.

NANTYCAFN COLLIERY HALT

This was the former name of what was later known as Dillwyn & Brynteg Platform and should be cross-referenced with Volume 1.

NANTYFFYN

Miners' stopping place situated between Bedlinog Colliery and Cwm Bargoed. In use by November 1928.

NANTYRONEN HALT

Situated on the narrow gauge Vale of Rheidol line between Capel Bagnor and Aberfrwd. Originally provided with a siding although this was removed around 1930. Not believed the 'Halt' suffix was ever displayed. Receipts included with those of Devils Bridge.

further reading: *The Vale of Rheidol Light Railway'*. Pub. Wild Swan.

NEACHEY HALT

see entry for Cosford Aerodrome Halt.

NEATH ENGINE SHED

Railwaymen's stopping place serving the shed of the same name and reported as located on the branch from Neath. In use by September 1928.

NETHERHOPE HALT

Located on the single line Wye Valley branch between Wye Junction and Tintern. Opened either 14 or 16 May 1932 with corrugated shelter, name and notice boards and path to road. (Other reports refer to construction having commenced in the spring of 1932 and the opening on an unspecified date in July 1932.) Shelter supplied by Messrs. Joseph Ash & Son Ltd of Birmingham.

further reading: *The Wye Valley Railway and the Coleford Branc'*. Pub. Oakwood Press.

The concrete shelter provided at Newbury West Fields Halt in 1906 and supplied by Messrs. S. Taylor & Co. of Birmingham. It was described as being of their patent 'universal roof covering and building material'. At least one other halt from the period, that at Cheltenham Race Course was similarly equipped. At an unreported date a conventional metal pagoda shelter was substituted.

National Railway Museum / GWR 'C' series 55779

NEWBURY RACECOURSE

Situated between Thatcham and Newbury stations. Opened on 26 September 1905 in connection with race-course traffic and having four platform faces fronting both loops and main line. During the period 1939-45, the building accommodation was used as railway staff living quarters.

NEWBURY WEST FIELDS HALT

Single platform situated on the east side of the Lambourn Valley branch between Newbury and Speen. Opened 1 October 1906 and originally provided with a low height platform 150ft. x 7ft. x 9ins. and typical of this line. The platform was raised to the standard height during 1908/9. From the outset a pagoda shelter was provided although this was unusual in that it was constructed of concrete. Receipts included with Lambourn under the corporate branch system.

further reading: *The Lambourn Branch*. Pub. Wild Swan.

NEW DALE HALT

On the Ketley branch between Ketley Town Halt and Horsehay & Dawley. Single platform provided, which opened on Monday 29 January 1934.

NEW HADLEY HALT

Situated between Wellington (Salop) and Oakengates. Authorised on 4 October 1934 with staggered up and down platforms 100ft. long, steps to public road, shelters, name and notice boards, gates and lighting. Estimated cost of £290. Opened to traffic on Saturday 3 November 1934.

NEW INN BRIDGE HALT

Single ash filled platform 75ft. long with shelter, 12ft. x 6ft. on the North Pembrokeshire & Fishguard line between Puncheston and Rosebush. Opened 14 October 1929 and illuminated by oil lamps.

New Hadley halt with its staggered timber platforms. Again there is a variant in the shelter design and it seems likely that by the 1930's at least locally available materials may well have been used if available.

Newland Halt and displaying again the thought to stopping places situated in close proximity to easy road access - see also photo of Mithian Halt on page 13. An extensive network of sidings was established here in the 1940's and these are depicted in the view on the next page.

Closed in October 1937. (There is some confusion with regard to a closure date with both the 15 and 25 of the same month being given although the latter is most likely.)

further reading: *The Railways of Pembrokeshire*. Pub. H.G. Waters.

NEWLAND HALT

Situated between Bransford Road and Malvern Link. Staggered up and down platforms provided. Opened 18 March 1929.

NEWLANDS COLLIERY PLATFORM

see entry for Newlands Halt.

NEWLANDS HALT

Situated on the former Port Talbot system between Morfa Crossing and Cribbwr Fawr. Opening date not reported. Renamed, Newlands Colliery Platform, by February 1930.

NEW PASSAGE HALT

Single platform with lighting and gates on the Avonmouth branch from Pilning. Authorised on 24 April 1928 under the heading 'Pilning Junction - Severn Beach, adapting line for passenger traffic'. Opened 9 July 1928. The estimated cost given, £502 included two other halts at Cross Hands and

The yard just south of Newland Halt on the Worcester and Hereford line. The wartime concrete-pot type sleepers will be noted.

National Railway Museum / GWR B.Box 397/42

Pilning on the same line. The original name for New Passage Halt was to have been Redwick Halt.

NEWPORT PILL

Unadvertised stopping place near the west end of the transporter at Newport ANSW, and used by munitions workers during the period 1914-18.

NEWPORT SOUTH DOCK

Unadvertised stopping place at the terminus of the ANSW line at Newport, used by munitions workers during the period 1914-18. Facilities consisted of a single long platform with wooden canopy.

NEW TREDEGAR COLLIERY HALT

see entry for New Tredegar Colliery Platform

NEW TREDEGAR COLLIERY PLATFORM

Situated between New Tredegar and McLaren Colliery. Staggered platforms brought into use by 1909 and in use until around July 1930 when a landslip severed the line. Also referred to as New Tredegar Colliery Halt.

NIGHTINGALE VALLEY HALT

Located on the single line Portishead branch between Ham Green Halt and Clifton Bridge. Opened on 9 July 1926 * and closed either on 23 September 1929 or from 12 September 1932. (The three year gap may refer to a time when the stopping place was in use during summer months only. Interestingly it appears only ever referred to be in the summer timetable but then it did serve a picnic spot only!)

GWR Traffic and Engineering Committee records differ considerably with regard to the opening date for this location. The former states the stopping place was authorised on 24 April 1928

with a single platform 400ft. x 8ft. with shelter, footpath and gate to road also lighting of an unspecified type. Estimated cost of £380 although this was exceeded by £16 16s 6d. An additional consideration is the opening date given by Clinker for the stopping place, which refers to 9 July 1928.)

further reading: *Reflections on the Portishead Branch*. Pub. OPC.

NINIAN PARK HALT

see entry for Ninian Park Platform

NINIAN PARK PLATFORM

Opened 2 November 1912 as a single platform some 300ft. long on the freight only Radyr to Cardiff General and Penarth line. As authorised it was to have been known as Leckwith Road Pleasure Platform but this decision was changed just before opening. A second platform face was added in 1932/3 and when the original was also lengthened by some 200ft. It was intended primarily for use of football traffic but was also used for seaside excursions on summer Saturdays from 1934 until 10 September 1939., these trains appearing in the public timetable. Sometimes referred to in official

records incorrectly as Nithian Park. Supervision exercised from Cardiff General.

NORTH ACTON HALT

Up and down platforms situated on the Acton & Northolt line between Old Oak Lane Halt and Park Royal. Opened 1 May 1904 and closed 1 February 1913. (A station with the similar name, North Acton, was opened in 1923 just east of the original halt.) Receipts for North Acton Halt were included with either Southall or Greenford stations.

NORTH FILTON PLATFORM

This stopping place was located between Filton Junction and Henbury on almost exactly the site of the previous Filton Halt. Opened 12 July 1926 with up and down platforms and parcels traffic handled. An entry in the official records for 5 October 1939 refers to, '...additional accommodation...', although no precise detail is given. The cost of this unspecified work at this time was reported as £315. See entries also for Filton Halt, and Gloucester Road Halt.

further reading: *'Bristol Railway Panorama'*. Pub. Millstream.

Opened in 1926 North Filton Platform is believed to have only ever possessed a single shelter. The confusion as regards the 1939 records entry continues! This was the scene on 17 August 1926 with Nos. 51134 / 51147 forming the 12.22 p.m. Bristol Temple Meads to Henbury on 17 August 1960.
H.B. Priestley

NORTHOLT HALT (FOR WEST END)

Situated on the Acton & Northolt line between South Ruislip and Greenford. Up and down platforms 100ft long complete with shelters either side. Opened 1 May 1907 and probably referred to as Northolt Halt. On 24 January 1929 additional facilities in the form of larger and wider platforms in concrete in place of the existing timber platforms and with new footpath approaches were authorised. Also a new corrugated iron booking office at road level. In addition, a new mileage siding on the up side and storing siding for rail-motors and auto-trains was included on the down side. Other changes included the provision of a cart weighbridge. The estimated cost of this work was £9,590. An upgrade to official station status followed from 23 September 1929. Although slightly out of context now it is worth recording that yet more new works were authorised on 17 March 1932 including the excavation and provision of new lavatories alongside the approach road and other minor work such as refixing a packers hut and steps. Electric lighting was also provided. This work was in connection with a scheme for improving the area rail-motor services and at an estimated cost of £741. Closed 21 November 1948.

further reading: *Great Western London Suburban Services*. Pub. Oakwood Press.

NORTH RHONDDA COLLIERY HALT

see entry for North Rhondda Halt.

NORTH RHONDDA HALT

Single platform able to accommodate just one bogie coach situated at the northern terminus of the South Wales mineral railway from Cymmer and brought into use from 23 August 1923. This was an unadvertised stopping place used by miners traffic and may also have gone under the name North Rhondda Colliery Halt. Around February 1930 the name Blaencorrwg Halt may also have been used. The platform itself was of timber construction and devoid of any shelter.

An illustration appears in, *Steam in South Wales Vol 1*. Plates 139/40. Pub. OPC

NORTHWOOD HALT

Single platform on the former Severn Valley line situated between Bewdley and Arley. Timber shelter provided and opened on Monday 17 June 1935.

NOTTAGE HALT

see entry for Porthcawl Golfers Platform.

Above and left ;
Northwood Halt captured on film probably just prior to opening in 1907. A point of interest is in the use of whitewash to identify the platforms edges, surely an unusual feature for the time. The large size running in boards and passenger information are in stark contrast to modern day passenger information. Whilst intended initially to serve what then a predominantly rural community, it is likely some additional traffic would have been generated with the establishment of the Northolt aerodrome in 1915 although at this time only in the form of service personnel. The need to supersede the basic facilities came about due to an ever expanding urban population whilst additionally there was also a racecourse served by the stopping place from 1929 although by this stage it had become a full station.
Both, Lens of Sutton.

Another 1930's built halt, this time at Northwood. The location survives almost exactly as built and continues to see steam services today as part of the Severn Valley route from Kidderminster to Bridgnorth.

Andrew Muckley

Halts were not always the province of the branch line as here at Oaksey between Kemble and Minety & Ashton Keynes.

OAKDALE HALT

Single platform served by both up and down trains and situated on the Penar branch north of Penmaen Halt. Opened 14 March 1927 following a GWR resolution of 9 October 1924 to adapt the Penar branch for passenger traffic. Facilities included platform with ramp at either end, corrugated iron shelter, pathway and gate leading to the platform. Also retaining wall at the rear. The estimated cost of £1,710 included the cost of a loop line with the necessary connections to serve the new platform. Closed 12 September 1932.

OAKSEY HALT

Up platform 150ft. x 8ft. and down platform 150ft. x 10ft. situated on the original South Wales main line between Kemble and Minety & Ashton Keynes. Both platforms provided with waiting shelters and approach roads. Opened on 18 February 1929 at an estimated cost of £640.

OGBOURNE HORSE PLATFORM

Situated between Ogbourne and Marlborough on the former MSWJ system. As the name implies this was used for private horse traffic form June 1897 although there must also be some doubt as to whether the heading should really be Ogbourne Horse Siding as any platform would only have been used for horse traffic. No evidence is available to suggest if passengers were ever handled. Out of use by 1923.

further reading: *The Midland & South Western Junction Railway.* Pub. Wild Swan.

OGILVIE COLLIERY HALT

Unadvertised stopping place

situated north of Darren & Deri and Ogilvie Village Halt and on the east side of the single line. Believed first used in September 1926. May also have been referred to as Ogilvie Colliery Platform

illustration in: *Steam in South Wales Vol. 5.* Pub. West Railway Record Circle.

OGILVIE COLLIERY PLATFORM

see entry for Ogilvie Colliery Halt.

OGILVIE VILLAGE HALT

Single platform situated between Ogilvie Colliery Halt and Darren & Deri on the west side of the single line. Opened either Thursday 9 or Thursday 16 May 1935.

OLD DOCK HALT

see entry for Port Talbot Docks.

OLDFIELD PARK HALT

Situated between Bath and Twerton. Up and down platforms opened 18 February 1929. On 29 January 1930 provision of lavatory accommodation was authorised at an estimated cost of £249. The entry in official records at this later time refers to Oldfield Park Halt,

although no suffix appears to have been used in the timetable.

OLDFIELD PARK PLATFORM

see entry for Oldfield Park Halt.

OLD HILL HIGH STREET HALT

Situated between Old Hill and Darby End Halt. Up and down platforms opened 21 August 1905.

OLD OAK COMMON

Unadvertised platform used by railwaymen only and situated between Westbourne Park and Acton. Brought into use after 1905 and closed by November 1915. The information on this entry is taken from *Private and Untimetabled Stations, Halts and Stopping Places.* Pub Oakwood Press, but could this and the following entry refer to one and the same place?

OLD OAK LANE HALT

Authorised on 10 January 1906 with up and down platforms 150ft. long, shelters, footpaths and steps to the public road. Located on the Acton & Northolt line between Old Oak Common and North Acton and brought into use on 1 October

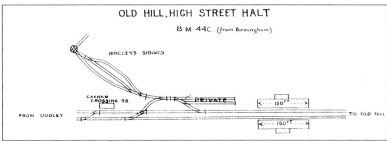

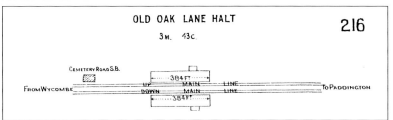

1906. At this time reference is intended, "...primarily for use of men engaged in the new locomotive depot at Old Oak Common". Cost of original facilities stated as £334. On 10 October 1906 lengthening of platforms authorised to 400ft, "...to enable trains to be accommodated." - but what then was accommodated previously? Temporary closure from 1 February 1915 and re-opened 30 March 1920. On 20 June 1932 a down bay line at the rear of the down platform was brought into use at a cost of £1,320, this was removed in November 1940. Receipts included with either Southall or Greenford. The location closed on 30 June 1947.

See also entry for Old Oak Common.

further reading: *Great Western London Suburban Services*. Pub. Oakwood Press.

OLDWOODS HALT

Located on the Shrewsbury to Chester line between Leaton and Baschurch. Up and down platforms 70ft x 8ft provided with shelters, booking office, footpath and steps to road, also access to neighbouring goods depot. Estimated cost of £279. Opening was not until 3 July 1933 although authorisation for the work had been given as far back as 27 April 1927.

OLD YNYSYBWL HALT

see entry for Old Ynysybwl Platform

OLD YNYSYBWL PLATFORM

Situated on the single track Ynysybwl branch between Ynysybwl and Llanwonno Colliery. This stopping place was the terminus of the railmotor service from Ponypridd / Abercynon. Opened on 1 November 1905 and renamed Old Ynysybwl Halt from 2 October 1922. Supervision exercised by the Ynysybwl Station Master.

illustration in: *Steam in South Wales Vol. 5*. Pub. West Railway Record Circle.

OLMARCH HALT

Single platform on the Carmarthen to Aberystwyth branch between Llangybi and Pont Llanio. Opened 7 December 1929.

54xx 0-6-0PT No. 5413 paused at Old Oak Lane Halt on a Greenford auto working sometime in the 1930's and coupled to trailer car No. 185, note the car carries a wooden destination board at waist level just beyond the centre door although this is not readable on the photograph.. The 54xx clas were a derivitive of the earlier '2021' design and were introduced from 1930 onwards as a replacement for the previous class. No. 5413 was built to Lot No. 277 and appeared from Swindon along with sister engines 5411-15 in May 1932. It may well be then that the engine was almost new when photographed. Auto-fitting was put on sometime between 1932-4. Of the 25 engines in the class two-thirds were initially allocated to Southall and from where motive power was provided for various suburban services. After electrification to Ruislip the class were more widely distributed and along with the similar but smaller wheeled 64xx and 74xx were to be found scattered throughout the system until branch line closures and the wholesale condemnation of steam rendered them redundant. No. 5413 one of seven of the class withdrawn in 1957.

Lens of Sutton.

Above: Old Oak Lane Halt looking east in 1931. The steam shed and carriage sidings were located out of sight to the left and with the main line also invisible but to the right. At this stage the bay platform had yet to be added but which would entail the removal of the fence on the right hand (down) platform.

L.G.R.P. 8995

Below: June 16 1947 and just two weeks before the steam services were withdrawn consequent upon the completion of the Central Line. The working is the 2.28 p.m. Northolt to Westbourne Park service and which is being propelled by No. 5401.

J.J. Smith

The quite remarkable scene at Pentrecourt Platform on the opening day of 1 February 1912, with upwards of 100 persons visible.
                                                                                    Great Western Trust

PADDINGTON GOODS

Situated on a branch from Westbourne Park and used by railwaymen from about 1905. Out of use by June 1915.

PANDY BRIDGE HALT

see entry for Rhosrobin Halt.

PANS LANE HALT

Single 208ft. platform situated on the west side of the line between Patney & Chirton and Devizes. Opened 4 March 1929. During the 1930s certain local services operating from Trowbridge terminated at Pans Lane before returning to Trowbridge.

further reading: *GWR to Devizes*. Pub. Millstream.

PANT HALT

Between Brook Street Halt and Wynn Hall Halt on the Llwynenion branch. Single platform opened 1 May 1905 and served by the GWR Wrexham to Wynn Hall passenger service. Closed 22 March 1915.

PANTYFFORDD HALT

Single platform between Seven Sisters and Onllwyn. Opened 2 September 1929 at a cost of £140.

PANTYSGALLOG HALT

Located on the Brecon and Dowlais branch between Pant and Dowlais (Central). Single platform opened 1 October 1910. (The LMSR also had a stopping place with the same name nearby and for this reason the location name was later altered to High Level.) Although strictly outside the scope of 'Great Western Halts', Pantysgallog perhaps has one small

Pans Lane Halt	Year	Tickets issued	Season Tickets	Total Receipts £
	1929	1476		83
	1930	1247		81
	1931	1454		86
	1932	1258		63
	1933	672	2	54

Pans Lane Halt just south of Devizes and depicted in its last week of operation. Originally provided to serve the County Mental Hospital the location was never very busy although later when housing had been developed in the vicinity a number of longer distance trains would call upon 'notice' being given to the guard. The train depicted is the 10.40 Devizes to Patney on 9 April 1966.

Paul Strong

The bleak outlook at Pantywaun Halt on 24 May 1958 with 56xx No. 5615 in charge of a four coach set.   *GWT*

Park Hall Halt viewed towards Oswestry and an example of where the available double track width has been put to good use for the provision of the platform. Examples of this type were to be found at numerous sites where halts were provided.

The original Parson Street Platform as existed between 1927 and 1933. After this date additional loops were provided and it was re-graded as a station. Although out of context a delightful story of the location from WW2 is worth recounting. It is said that the driver of a Taunton to Bristol goods told his guard that he should ignore a stop at what was then Parson Street Station. When the train drew up there, the guard saw the driver climb in the 'station truck' behind the engine and roll a cheese, then rationed, down the embankment to his home. An anthill diverted the cheese into a neighbour's greenhouse. To appease the neighbour's wrath, the driver agreed to share the cheese with him.   *Mowat Collec. M234.*

claim to fame not shared by any other GWR Halt. It is concerned with its closure. In the first place closure of the branch and its halt and terminus station to public passenger trains took place on 28 June 1952. However, workmen's services were destined to continue - and they did, advertised in the public timetable! These services were finally announced as being withdrawn from 2 May 1960, but it seems nobody thought to advise Dowlais, for trains continued to run - empty - for another week!

PANTYWAUN HALT

Staffed stopping place on the Bargoed and Pant single line between Dowlais Top and Fochriw. Opened 22 December 1941 and not believed provided with any shelter. In some respects this is understandable as from the village it served, trains could he heard approaching for several minutes.

PAR BRIDGE

Unadvertised stopping place between St. Blazey and Fowey and reported as in use on summer Wednesdays only by July 1897. Out of use sometime after 1902.

PARCYRHUN HALT

Single platform situated between Pantyffyron and Tirydail. Authorised on 13 February 1936 at an estimated cost of £170, and opened 4 May 1936.

PARK HALL HALT

Situated between Oswestry and Gobowen. Single platform provided. Opened 5 July 1926. On 25 July 1935 an extension of the platform and provision of a shelter was authorised at a cost of £140.

further reading: *Great Western Journal. No. 22.* Pub. Wild Swan.

PARK ROYAL

Situated between North Acton Halt and Twyford Abbey. Opened 15 June 1903 to serve a showground closed 5 July 1903. The site was later reopened on 1 May 1904 as a public station and which itself closed on 26 September 1937

further reading: *Great Western London Suburban Services.* Pub. Oakwood Press.

PARSON STREET PLATFORM

Situated between Bedminster and Portishead Junction. Parcels traffic handled. Up and down platforms opened 29 August 1927. On 6 June 1929 plans were made for improvements including: 'Extension of Booking Office - £66, works for lavatory accommodation, excavation, retaining wall, lavatory, fittings, drainage and water supply - £72, Removing building from Monckton Combe, making good and re-erecting at Parson Street to serve as a lavatory building - £204, Refixing W/C from Dunkerton - £5, Electric lighting - £15'. An additional note then stated, 'Scheme abandoned as halt will be reconstructed with government development scheme'. The stopping place was re-classified as a station in November 1933 with additional loop platforms and presumably was then rebuilt at this time. The term Platform was also dropped from then on.

PAULTON HALT

Situated on the single line Camerton branch between Hallatrow and Radford & Timsbury Halt. Opened on 5 January 1914 with standard height platform 151ft. x 8ft. and likely to have also had a shelter. Receipts included with Hallatrow station. Public access was via a footbridge leading to the road from Clutton. The stopping place was subject to temporary closure from 22 March 1915 to 9 July 1923. Permanent closure from 21 September 1925.

further reading: *The Camerton Branch.* Pub. Wild Swan.

PEBWORTH HALT

On the double track main line between Honeybourne and Long

Marston. Up and down platforms 150ft. x 8ft. with shelters, gates, steps to road, oil hut and lighting. Authorised at an estimated cost of £430 on 29 April 1937 and opened on 6 September 1937. This stopping place was some 352 yards south of the site of the former Broad Marston Halt which closed in 1916 - see Volume 1.

further reading: *The Stratford on Avon to Cheltenham Railway.* Pub. Irwell Press.

PEDAIR FFORD

Situated between Lalnrhaiadr and Penybontfawr on the Tanat Valley branch. Opened 6 January 1904 with a single timber platform on the up side and provided with a lean-to corrugated shelter open at the front.

further reading: *The Tanat Valley Light Railway.* Pub. Wild Swan.

PEMBREY HALT

Situated between Burry Port and Trimsaran Road. Single masonry platform provided with corrugated shelter and opened 2 August 1909 with access from the nearby road over-bridge. The suffix was dropped shortly afterwards but

restored again by the GWR from 1 July 1924.

PENALLT HALT

Single timber platform and round topped corrugated shelter on the Wye Valley branch located between Redbrook-on-Wye and Whitebrook Halt. Opened 1 August 1931 being given. See entry also for Netherhope Halt.

further reading: The Wye Valley Railway and the Coleford Branch. Pub. Oakwood Press.

PENAR JUNCTION HALT

Up and down platforms situated on the Vale of Neath line between Penttwynawr and Pontllanfraith. Opened 1 May 1913 and closed on 1 January 1917 although still intact several years later. Possibly then a re-opening was envisaged although that would never occur. (The GWR Magazine for 1913 refers to "...the provision of a Halt at Penner Junction...during 1912." This was the original name of the nearby junction although it was changed at an unreported date to Penar junction. It is possible then that originally the stopping place was first known as Penner Junction Halt.)

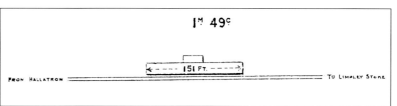

Regretfully there a number of locations and which for a variety of reasons do not appear to have attracted the attention of the photographer in their heyday. One of these is Paulton Halt, seen here towards the end but remarkably still with the remains of the nameboard intact.

The pedestrain access to Pebworth Halt in later years. Whilst in no way could the mass of timber be considered to have been designed to follow a particular architectural styling, it was functional, cheap to produce and accordingly cost effective. Clearly though it also would only ever have been accessible to able bodied individuals as well.   *D.J. Hyde*

Pedair Ffordd Halt in 1904. The nameboard displays the location as a single word and no suffix is displayed, by no means untypical of the records compared with the practical, and appertaining to several locations. The facilities remained basically unaltered throughout the life of the location and were also typical of those to be found on the Tanat Valley Railway.   *L.G.R.P.*

PENARTH HALT

Unadvertised stopping place located between Abermule and Newtown. Single platform only provided.

PENCARREG HALT

Single platform on the Camarthen to Aberystwyth branch between Lampeter and Llanybyther. Opened 9 June 1930.

PENHELIG HALT

Single part masonry, part timber platform situated on the up side of the line between Aberdovey and Abertafol Halt. Authorised on 9 February 1933 and opened 8 May 1933 with an unusual timber pagoda style building. Public access being via footpath and steps leading up from houses below the level of the railway embankment. Estimated cost of £320. (The halt actually stood between Aberdovey No. 3 and No. 4 tunnels.)

further reading: *The Coast Lines of the Cambrian Railway Vol. 2*. Pub. Wild Swan.

PENMAEN HALT

Situated between Pentwynmawr and Oakdale Halt. Authorised on 9 October 1924 although not opened until sometime between 9 and 14 March 1927 with staggered up and down platforms 150ft. long with ramps and shelters. Estimated cost of £955. Closed 25 September 1939.

PENMAWR & OAKDALE HALT

This is an entry for a location which according to O.S. Nock, opened on 11 July 1927. No details as to location are given, and the name fails to appear in any other listing or atlas.

PENMERE PLATFORM

Single platform 300ft. long with ramps, booking office, waiting shed, pathway and gate. Situated between Penryn and Falmouth. Authorised on 9 October 1924, '...to serve a large housing estate in the course of development...'. Estimated cost of the work and facilities £854. Opened either 1 June or 1 July 1925. The original intention was to call the stopping place 'Penmere Halt'. On 26 January 1928 an additional ladies' waiting room and lavatories for both ladies and gents adjacent to the existing buildings were authorised. The estimated cost of this work was £300.

PENNER JUNCTION HALT

see entry for Penar Junction Halt.

PENN HALT

Situated on the Kingswinford branch between Wombourn and Tettenhall. Standard height platform 250ft. long with 20ft. x 8ft. corrugated pagoda shelter,

PENAR JUNCTION HALT
8 M. 15 C.
(NOT IN USE)

FROM SWANSEA   350 FT
UP   MAIN   LINE
DOWN   MAIN   LINE   TO PONTYPOOL ROAD
350 FT

Penallt Halt in the Wye Valley and facing towards Monmouth, 3 January 1959.   *J. Dagley-Morris*

Pencarreg Halt on the Camarthen to Aberystwyth branch between Lampeter and Llanybyther. The finger post identified the path from the road and it is likely that there were at some other dwellings to provide traffic other than the single one seen. The facilities were on the east side of the running line and some 8 miles 42 chains from Pencader Junction.   *Austin Attewell*

Penmere Platform in August 1948 and with what could be No. 5537 approaching. The line on the left served as a headshunt to some oil sidings south west of the location. On 12 January 1941 a landslip occurred near the stopping place and caused the derailment of the branch train fortunately without causing serious injury.

Joe Moss / Roger Carpenter

Two views of Penhelig Halt in 1935 and when it had been in existence for just over two years. The reference in the text to the location being between the tunnels is also clearly explained. The open framework to the platform will be noted except that underneath the shelter and which in itself of unusual manufacture - the small extension being a ticket office. It would be perhaps unwise to refer to its wooden construction as unique but it must certainly be unusual. Could it even have been due to the presence of salt in the wind from the nearby estuary likely to corrode a steel structure, or was passenger comfort the major consideration?

National Railway Museum / GWR 'B' Box 285/19 & 285/20

lamp hut and footpath to the public road which crossed the railway at the Himley end of the stopping place. Opened 11 May 1925 (although plans for the stopping place have been found dated as early as 11 April 1911) and originally intended to have been called Upper and Lower Penn Halt. A lamp hut was sited at track level at the opposite end of the platform to the footpath. Closed 31 October 1932.

further reading: *The Railway to Wombourn*. Pub. Uralia Press.

PENPONT HALT

see entry for Penpont Platform

PENPONT PLATFORM

Private stopping place with a single platform 63ft. long situated between Aberbran and Abercamlais Halt. Opened by February 1920 with the name changed at an unknown date to Penpont Halt.

PENSCYNOR HALT

Single timber platform and pagoda shelter situated between Cilfrew and Cadoxton Terrace Halt. Opened 1 August 1929.

PENSNETT HALT

Situated between Brettell Lane and Himley. Originally a station although downgraded to Halt status from 11 May 1925. Facilities included up and down platforms, an open footbridge and at least one arc-roofed corrugated shelter. It is not known if the Halt suffix was carried. Closed 31 October 1932.

further reading: *The Railway to Wombourn*. Pub. Uralia Press.

PENTRE BROUGHTON HALT

Single platform situated on the down side of the Moss Valley branch between Gatewen Halt and Gwersyllt Halt. No shelter provided and unstaffed. The train guard attended to lighting and extinguished the lamps as required. Opened 1 May 1905 and closed from 1 January 1931.

PENTRECOURT PLATFORM

Situated between Llandyssul and Henllan on the branch to Newcastle Emlyn. Single 200' platform provided. Opened 1 February 1912. Also referred to as Pentrecourt Halt. Corrugated shelter and two oil lamps which were attended to daily by the lad porter from Llandysul who also carried out general housekeeping duties at the location before returning to his home station by the next service train.

further reading: *Great Western Journal. No. 37.* Pub. Wild Swan.

PENTREFELIN

Situated between Llangedwyn and Llananrhaiadr Mochnant on the Tanat Valley Branch. A siding was provided opposite the platform, the latter having a small shelter.

further reading: *The Tanat Valley Light Railway.* Pub. Wild Swan.

PENTREFELIN (GLAM) HALT

see entry for Pentrefelin Halt

PENTREFELIN HALT

Situated between Morriston (West) and Felin Fran Halt. Authorised on 16 February 1928 with up and down timber platforms 120ft. long, pathway to bridge, booking hut and gate. Estimated cost of £395. Opened 16 April 1928. In the public timetable this stopping place was referred to as Pentrefelin (Glam) Halt, to avoid obvious confusion with the previous entry.

PENTREMAWR COLLIERY SIDING

Unadvertised stopping place situated on the former BPGV system between Pontyberem and Pont Henry. Used by miners from 1913 onwards.

PENTREPIOD HALT

Situated between Abersychan and Pontypool Crane Street. Although the earliest known plan for the location is dated 23 October 1907, the stopping place was not authorised until 23 February 1911

Pentrefelin Halt and close to the site of what once been the site of the colliery of the same name. A further colliery had also once existed a short distance of the east of the location and known as Bryn Whilach Colliery. Both had ceased operations prior to 1947. Mowat Collec. M924

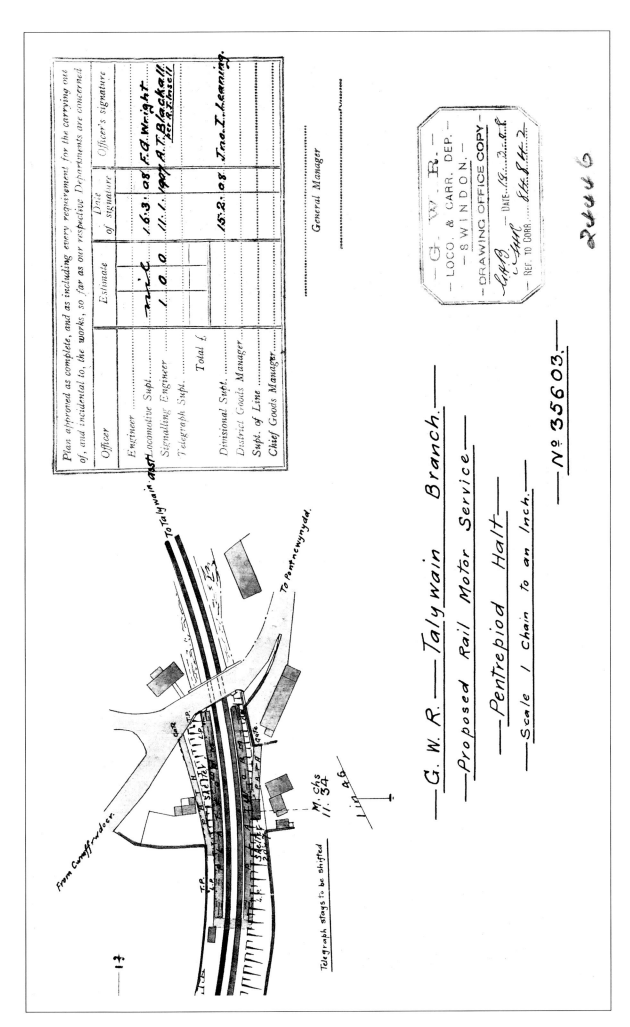

Plan approved as complete, and as including every requirement for the carrying out of, and incidental to, the works, so far as our respective Departments are concerned

Officer	Estimate	Date of signature	Officer's signature
Engineer	nil	1.6.3. 08	F.G. Wright.
Asst. Locomotive Supt.	1. 0. 0.	11.1. 1909	A.T. Blackall. per R. Ibbsell
Signalling Engineer			
Telegraph Supt.			
Total £			
Divisional Supt.		15.2. 08	Ino. I. Leaning.
District Goods Manager			
Supt. of Line			
Chief Goods Manager			

.... General Manager

— G. W. R. — Talywain Branch. —

— Proposed Rail Motor Service —

— Pentrepiod Halt —

— Scale 1 Chain to an Inch —

— Nº 35603. —

To Talywain.

To Pontnewynydd.

From Cwmffrwdoer.

M. Chs
11. 34

Telegraph stays to be shifted

at an estimated cost of £438. Up and down platforms 150ft. long provided and opened on 12 July 1912. Although a board crossing was provided at the Newport end of the site access to both platforms was also available via pathways leading to an over bridge at the Talywain end. Closed 5 May 1941. in official records Pentre Piod Halt was used but this spelling never appeared in the public timetables.

PENTRE PLATFORM

Situated on the former Taff Vale system and provided with up and down platforms. Closure date uncertain although ceased to appear in timetables from November 1912.

PENTRE SAESON HALT

Situated between Brymbo and Coed Poeth. Single timber platform provided on the up side of the line surmounted by a corrugated iron booking hut and shelter. Normally unstaffed although in 1924 it was the practice for a porter from Wrexham to attend to the booking of passengers on Saturdays.

Opened 20 March 1905 and closed on 1 January 1931.

PENWYN HALT

Situated between Abersychan and Talywain and Pentre Piod Halt. This was one of three halts on the Eastern Valleys line authorised on 23 February 1911, the others being at Cwmffrwdoer, and Pentrepiod Halt. Facilities consisted of up and down masonry platforms 150ft. long and provided at an estimated cost of £495. Opened 13 July 1912. Closed 5 May 1941.

PENTWYNMAWR PLATFORM

On the Vale of Neath line with up and down platforms and shelters provided. Opened 8 February 1926. Situated between Crumlin High Level and Pontllanfraith. Staffed and with parcels traffic also handled. The suffix was not shown on the nameboards.

PENYCHAIN HALT

Situated between Abererch and Afon Wen on the former Cambrian

line to Pwllheli. Authorised on 25 May 1933 at an estimated cost of £125. Single platform provided and opened on 31 July 1933. During the period 1939 to 1947 the stopping place was used by service personnel stationed at shore establishment 'HMS Glendower' - later the Pwllheli Butlin's holiday camp. An entry for 31 January 1941 refers to, '...an extension of the facilities for the use of the Admiralty - £350.' Further details of this work are not given. After 3 April 1947 the stopping place was upgraded to station status and the Halt suffix was dropped. In consequence a second platform was installed and the original platform lengthened.

further reading: *The Cambrian Coast Railway.* Pub. Foxline.

PENYDARREN PLATFORM

Situated on the GWR Rhymney line between Cwm Bargoed and Dowlais Cae Harris. Unadvertised, but with up and down platforms. In use by miners from about September 1928.

PERIVALE HALT

Situated between Park Royal and Greenford. Up and down platforms 391ft. long opened on 1 May 1904.

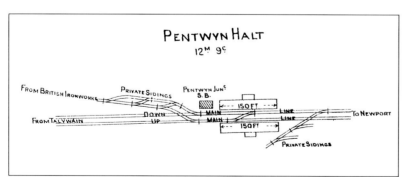

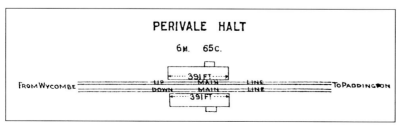

Opposite page: Perivale Halt viewed towards London. As with the early view of Old Oak Lane Halt, the location was somewhat rural in the early days although industry was soon to arrive in the shape of sidings for Sandersons (wallpaper), Bulmers, and the Electro-Metallic Recovery Company. Later to the Central Line would build a station alongside the GWR. The accommodation again displays differences to the standard pagoda, no least of which are the castellations. Did this indicate a wealthy clientele!

National Railway Museum / GWR

Temporary closure 1 February 1915 to 29 March 1920. Receipts included with either Southall or Greenford. Suffix dropped from 10 July 1922 although on 30 October 1930 improvements were authorised at Perivale Halt as follows: 'Extension of shelters on up and down sides and provision of additional covering and urinal on up side - £177. New ticket collectors office on down side - £28. New and enlarged booking office in lieu of existing to be removed. Additional work - £187. Electric lighting - £130.' Closed either 15 or 30 June 1947.

further reading: *Great Western London Suburban Services.* Pub. Oakwood Press.

PERRANPORTH BEACH HALT

Located on the single track Chacewater and Newquay line between Mithian Halt and Perranporth. Authorised on 30 April 1931 at an estimated cost of £720. Opened on 20 July 1931 although the entry in official Engineering Committee records referring to the stopping place does not appear until 30 April 1932, and a full year after the same reference appeared with the Traffic Committee! Besides the single platform, facilities included a waiting room, booking office, electric lighting and approach road. The estimated cost of the stopping place was £720. On 10 December 1948 approval was given for the renewal of the platforms and buildings in concrete at an estimated cost of £2,200. Electric lighting was also to be installed for a further £200. Shortly afterwards on 18 December 1948 additional expenditure on lavatory accommodation was approved for an estimated £405. Staffed only during the summer months and referred to in the RCH 'Handbook of Stations' as Perranporth Beach Platform'.

Perranporth Beach Halt and which was the last of the intermediate locations on the Chacewater & Newquay line. (The other halts on the line dated from 1905.) Accordingly the concrete structure may originate from that time.

further reading: *The Newquay Branch.* Pub. OPC

PERRANPORTH BEACH PLATFORM

see entry for Perranporth Beach Halt.

PICKHILL HALT

On the Wrexham and Ellesmere

Pilning low Level recorded about 1930. The similarly named Pilning High level was just a few yards distance and located parallel and behind the signal box. Mowat Collec. 218

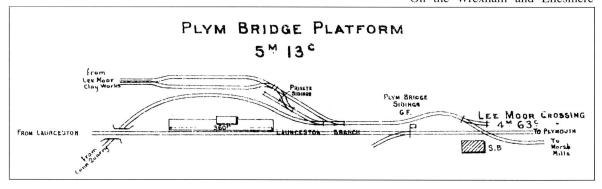

Line between Sesswick Halt and Bangor-on-Dee. Single platform opened 30 May 1938. Temporary closure from 10 June 1940 to 6 May 1946.

PILNING HALT

Situated between Pilning Junction and Severn Beach. This was on the site of the very first station at Pilning, which closed in 1886. Re-opened then as a Halt on 9 July 1928 with a single platform and gates to the road having been authorised on 24 April 1928 at the same time as New Passage Halt, both under the reference 'Pilning Junction - Severn Beach, adapting line for passenger traffic.' Referred to in the 1928 register as Pilning Halt although the reference Pilning Low Level appears to have been widely used and it is was this latter reference that appeared in the public timetable. (Pilning Low Level halt appeared on tickets issued there.) It is not believed that any form of lighting was at first provided. The estimated cost of £502 refers to the three locations, Pilning, Cross Hands, and New Passage Halts.

further reading: *Bristol Railway Panorama*. Pub. Millstream.

PILNING LOW LEVEL

see entry for Pilning Halt.

PINEWOOD HALT

On the northern section (Didcot - Newbury) of the former DN&S line between Hampstead Norris and Hermitage stations. Single platform with corrugated pagoda shelter on the west side of the line and opened on 11 September 1933. Temporary closure from 4 August 1942 to 8 March 1943 during which time a double track was laid between Didcot and Newbury. In consequence, the original platform was cut back slightly and a second platform with identical facilities erected opposite to serve the new down line. Public access was via pathways leading from a nearby brick over bridge. Receipts included with Hermitage.

further reading: *The Didcot, Newbury & Southampton Railway.* Pub. Wild Swan.

PINGOED HALT

Single platform situated between Burry Port and Trimsaren Road. Opened 2 August 1909 with the above name, but the suffix was later dropped. Restored by the GWR from 2 October 1922.

PLAS-Y-COURT HALT

On the Shrewsbury and Welshpool branch between Breiddon and Welshpool. Single platform opened 3 November 1934.

PLYM BRIDGE HALT

Situated between Marsh mills and Bickleigh. Single platform 360ft. long with shelter on the down side of the line and opened on 1 May 1906. (In May 1949 the length of the platform was reduced by 100ft.)

further reading: *The Tavistock, Launceston and Princetown Railways.* Pub. Oakwood Press.

PLYMOUTH DOCKS

Unadvertised stopping place

Plym Bridge Halt - the term platform appears to have been used with equal regard. From the photograph then view would tend to presence an appearance of serene tranquillity, although as can be seen from the plan opposite there was considerable industry within close proximity.

L.G.R.P. 7832

located beyond Millbay station and used by boat trains from June 1878. The location was later known as the Ocean Terminal.

PONKEY CROSSING HALT

On the Ponkey branch between Gardden Lodge Junction and Aberderfyn and the terminus of the passenger service from Wrexham. This was via Legacy on the Legacy to Ruabon line. Opened 5 June 1905 and closed on 22 March 1915.

PONTCYNON BRIDGE HALT

see entry for Pontycynon Bridge Platform.

PONTCYNON BRIDGE PLATFORM

see entry for Pontycynon Bridge Platform.

PONTHENRY

Between Pontyates and Pontyberem on the Burry Port to Cwmawr line. The status is unclear as it apparently opened on 2 August 1909 as a Halt - and is given this status by Bradshaw in 1910. However, by 1922 it had achieved full station status.

PONTHENRY COLLIERY SIDING

Single platform used by miners on the former BPGV line between Ponthenry and Pontremawr Colliery. In use by 1909.

PONTLOTTYN COLLIERY HALT

Unadvertised miners stopping place on the former Rhymney Railway between Tir Phil and Pontlottyn. Island platform in use from 1 January 1916 and closed by September 1928. May also have been known as Pontlottyn Colliery Platform.

PONTLOTTYN COLLEIRY PLATFORM

see entry for Pontlottyn Colliery Halt.

PONTNEWYDD HALT

Single platform situated between Trimsaren Road and Pontyates on the former BPGV line. Opened 2 August 1909 and renamed Glyn Abbey circa November 1910. This was due to parcels and other goods incorrectly being despatched to the stopping place and which should have been sent to Pontnewydd station in Monmouthshire. Possibly the Halt status was dropped around the same time. Then became Glyn Valley Halt from either 1 August 1942 or 3 May 1943.

PONTRHYDYRUN HALT

Authorised on 23 March 1933 at an estimated cost of £455 and located between Sebastapol and Upper Pontnewydd. Timber up and down platforms 150ft. x 8ft. provided with round-top corrugated shelters, footpaths, steps to road, oil hut, fencing and gates. The estimated cost of the facilities was put at £385 plus a further £70 for electric lighting. Opened on 17 July 1933. The stopping place was some 480 yards south of the site of the former Pontrhydyrun station, which had closed in 1917.

PONTSARN HALT

Formerly a station located between Cefn Coed and Pontsticill Junction. Single platform with substantial wooden buildings reduced in status from 1 March 1934.

PONTWALBY HALT

Situated between British Rhondda Halt and Rhigos Halt on the Vale of Neath line. This stopping place was authorised on 26 May 1910 under the following entry, 'Pontwalby - removal of the halt at British Rhondda and refixing it here. £424.' Up and down platforms 200ft. long provided, with shelters, and opened on 1 May 1911. The reference to British Rhondda Halt is particularly interesting (see Volume 1), for the latter stopping

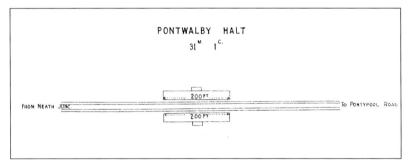

Pontycynon Bridge Platform (sic), another of the small stopping places provided by the Taff Vale Railway and with its origins dating back to 1905. It is depicted here in in June 1962 albeit no doubt in much modified form from what was originally provided.. M. Hale

place is reported as only possessing a single platform whilst its closure date is likewise given as 1 May 1911.) Note, British Rhondda Halt like Maindy Halt was the terminus of a railmotor service which, once reloaded, returned down the valley by means of a cross-over. It was situated immediately south of Pontwalby viaduct. Pontwalby Halt was immediately north of the viaduct and consisted of one wooden platform, presumably ex-British Rhondda and one masonry or ash filled platform.)

PONTYBEREM

Situated between Ponthenry and Cwmmawr on the BPGV system and opened as an unadvertised stopping place for use of miners in 1898. At this time only a single platform was provided. On 2 August 1909 it was re-classified as a public station, and then in October 1912 a second platform was provided.

PONTYCYNON BRIDGE HALT

see entry for Pontycynon Bridge Platform

PONTYCYNON BRIDGE PLATFORM

Single platform situated on the former Taff Vale system between Abercynon and Matthewstown Halt. First appeared in the public timetable in January 1905. Spelling altered to Pontcynon Bridge Platform from January 1910. Renamed Pontcynon Bridge Halt from 2 October 1922.

PONTGWAITH HALT

'Up' and 'down' platforms located between Quakers Yard and Merthyr Vale Junction. Opened 11 September 1933.

PONTGWAITH PLATFORM

Situated on the Taff Vale system between Tylorstown and Ynyshir. Up and down platforms provided, and opened 5 June 1905. Closed 1

Pontypridd Tram Road Halt and recorded in the year of closure, 1922. The location possessed just a single platform and with the major route from Treforest to Pontypridd seen at the end of the platform running left to right.
L.G.R.P. 18551

The stopping place at Portcawl Golfers Platform although known as Nottage Halt by the time the view was taken in 1949. As will be appreciated it was originally private and this explains the design of the shelter. The photograph is looking north towards Pyle.

L.G.R.P. 19757

October 1914.

PONTYPOOL (BLAENDARE ROAD) HALT

See entry for Blaendare Road Halt.

PONTYPRIDD TRAM ROAD HALT

Inspected and opened for the "motor car service" between Pontypridd and Caerphilly on 1 September 1904. At that time it was a single platformed rail level halt with a small shelter and the usual gate which was opened by the conductor. However a further report

to the Board of Trade dated 28 April 1906 states that the old halt had been replaced by a platform 100ft. x 10ft., being 3ft.6ins. above rail level and that the old shelter had been extended with ladies waiting room and convenience added along with additional lighting. The locked gate arrangement, however, continued and suggesting there were no staff in full time attendance. Closed 10 July 1922.

PORTBURY SHIPYARD PLATFORM

Located between Pill and Portishead. Opened for use of

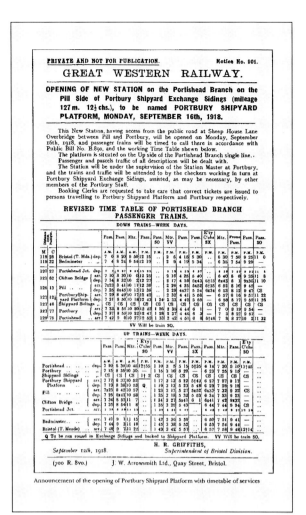

Announcement of the opening of Portbury Shipyard Platform with timetable of services

workers on 16 September 1918 and closed 26 March 1923.

further reading: *Bristol Railway Panorama.* Pub. Millstream, and *Reflections on the Portishead Branch.* Pub. OPC.

PORTHCAWL GOLFERS PLATFORM

Single platform situated between Pyle and Porthcawl. In use privately from about July 1902 to 14 July 1924. From 22 September 1924 appeared in the passenger timetables as a public stopping place with the name Nottage Halt. Masonry platform and non-standard shelter provided.

PORTOBELLO HALT

This was a 1911 proposal by the Cardiff Railway for a stopping place between Tongwynlais and Glan-y-Llyn. It was not proceeded with.

PORT SUNLIGHT HALT

Located on the joint LNWR/GWR

Portbury Shipyard Platform and which was in use solely for five years between 1918 and 1923. The platform was on the north side of what was a single line branch although there was a loop just over a quarter of a mile long at the end of the site and as per the signals.
Collec. M. Tozer

line from Spital to Bebington & New Ferry. Authorised by the GWR on 30 October 1913 and intended for use of employees of Lever Bros. Up and down platforms provided at an estimated cost of £1,500. Used by workmen from 1 May 1914 to 9 May 1927. Had also been used for a Royal Visit on 25 March 1914. Became a public station from 11 July 1927.

PORT TALBOT DOCKS

Situated on the RSBR branch from Aberavon Town. Previously a public station but from 14 March 1895 only used by workmen. Single platform 341ft. in length provided. May also have been known as Port Talbot Old Dock Halt. Out of use by 1947.

PORT TALBOT OLD DOCK HALT

see entry for Port Talbot Docks.

POTTERY SIDING

Workmen's stopping place located between Highbridge and Dunball. Dates of opening and closure not reported although known to have been in use in January 1917.

POYLE ESTATE HALT

Single platform on the Staines (West) branch serving an industrial estate.

POYLE HALT FOR STANWELL MOOR.

Situated between West Drayton and Staines. Single platform opened on 1 June 1927. Referred to in public timetables as 'Poyle, for Stanwell Moor, Halt.' Receipts included with Staines.

PRESCOTT SIDING

Single low height platform 62ft. long situated between Cleobury Town and Stottesdon and although a corrugated goods shed was provided there was no shelter for passengers. Parcels traffic handled. Classified by the GWR as a halt although the suffix was not carried.

Closed to passengers 26 September 1938 and entirely from 11 September 1939.

further reading: *The Cleobury Mortimer & Ditton Priors Railway.* Pub. OPC.

PRESTON PLATFORM

Up and down platforms 300ft. x 8ft. located on the Torquay branch between Torquay and Paignton. References to the stopping place first appear in the Engineering Committee Minutes in June 1911 although it was obviously considered before this as the construction contract is dated 22 May 1911 with the work scheduled for completion by 1 July 1911. Opening took place on 24 July 1911. The estimated cost of the stopping place was £965 with facilities including, '...alcoves, office on up side, steps and pathway', access between the platforms being via the public road under the railway at this point. Construction was undertaken by an outside contractor, Messrs. C.H. Hunt & Sons of Station Works, High Wycombe for a contract price of £840, although this was

exceeded by £30. The original GWR reference refers to Preston Sands Halt, and which may then be assumed to be the originally intended name. The contract also confirms a number of interesting features, including that Messrs. Hunt & Sons were responsible for the provision, construction and painting of the basic stopping place with the GWR providing the 'standard items', such as the corrugated huts (one 30ft. x 9ft. and the other 20ft. x 9ft.) lamps, nameboards etc, and which were then erected by the contractor. Closed 21 September 1914.

further reading, *The Newton Abbot to Kingswear Railway.* Pub. Oakwood Press.

PRESTON SANDS HALT

see entry for Preston Platform

PRITCHARD SIDING

Workmen's stopping place located between Briton Ferry Road and Swansea East Dock. Opened by July 1915 and in use until at least October 1920. The reported location is very close to the former

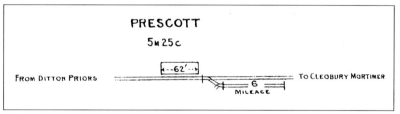

PRESCOTT
5M 25c

FROM DITTON PRIORS   62'   TO CLEOBURY MORTIMER
6
MILEAGE

Poyle Halt. Dating from 1927 this was one of the London division halts that failed to develop traffic as perhaps had been expected. Its basic facilities remained unaltered until 1964, when on 5 October of that year the shelter was destroyed in a fire. It was not replaced.

Collec. D.J. Hyde

Baldwins Halt (see Volume 1) and it may well have been that these were in fact one and the same with a name change taking place.

PROBUS & LACOCK PLATFORM

Situated between Grampound Road and Truro. Up and down timber platforms provided with corrugated pagoda shelters and which were known to have been elongated in the late 1920's. Three staff were provided including a Station Master - possibly a unique grading for a stopping place with Platform status. Opened on 1 February 1908.

Probus & Lacock Platform on the main line of the former Cornwall Railway and some 295 miles 47 chains from Paddington. In so far as the main line was concerned this was the most westerly of all the halts and platforms on the GWR although others did of course exist on the various Cornish branch lines. The extensive facilities that existed are clearly illustrated and which include yet another variant on the pagoda shelter design. Despite the provision of staff and the handling of parcels, goods traffic was not dealt with.

A brief look also at the traffic handled over the years is in many ways a sad reflection of the changing traffic patterns on the railways generally. In 1913 for example, 9063 tickets were issued and 3032 parcels dealt with.. This provided for a total revenue of £827 offset against which were direct pay bill expences for the three staff of £98. No figures are given for building and / or site maintenance nor the proportion to be offset for locomotive and rolling stock costs. Even so the location displayed a healthy profit. By 1923 though and still with three staff, station wages had risen to £381 against £656 revenue for passengers and parcels. The worst year for which figures are available was probably 1932 and with staff costs at £385 and total receipts of £392. A gross profit of just £7 for the year would probably have meant drastic economy or even closure had it continued, but fortunately these figures were not repeated and despite several 'hic-cups' along the way a degree of profitability had been restored by 1938 with £374 in salaries and wages compared to £563 for receipts. Interestingly also the location issued a number of season tickets annually although of these the most issued was only 17 in 1933. Parcels traffic in so far as volume was concerned had also peaked in 1913 and by 1923 had fallen by almost two-thirds. The 1913 figure for parcels only exceeded once in the next 25 years and this in 1938 when 3143 items were reported as dealt with. There is no distinction given for pieces sent or received in the available figures. Returning again finally to the number of passenger tickets sold and with the fall in revenue was most marked. From a huge peak of over 9063 tickets issued in 1913 it was down to just 545 by 1938 and indicative then of changing traffic patterns in the form of local road competition.

L.G.R.P. 8799

QUATFORD HALT

Proposed halt on the ill-fated and never-built, Wolverhampton - Bridgenorth line.

further reading: *The Railway to Wombourn*. Pub. Uralia Press.

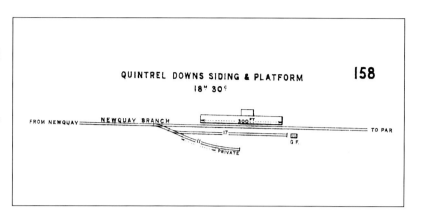

QUINTREL DOWNS PLATFORM

Single platform 300ft. long with shelter on the line between Newquay and St. Columb Road. The stopping place was first referred to as "proposed" in the GWR Magazine for June 1911, and was opened on 2 October 1911, no details of cost being given. Opposite the platform was a goods siding controlled by a ground frame. The ground frame was moved to a new location atop the platform sometime after 1922.

further reading: *The Newquay Branch*. Pub. OPC

Below:

Quintrel Downs depicted in 1922 and viewed towards Newquay. It is likely that this photograoh shows the site almost as built although considerable change would take place later with the removal of the levers within the ground frame to a new location inside the pagoda and which was then moved to a new location on the platform and closer to the camera. This can be seen from the top view on the next page.

L.G.R.P. 8831

Quintrel Downs in later years and with the pagoda having been resited and serving as both waiting shelter and ground frame.

The halt at Radford and Timsbury and probably depicted around the time of opening, 9 May 1910 and the Camerton - Limpley Stoke line. No. 562, a '517' class 0-4-2T is seen arriving from Limpley Stoke with a motor train. According to the Wild Swan book on the Camerton Branch, the platform at the halt was not constructed in accordance with then Board of Trade requirements in that it did not have the requisite 12 inch overhang. Colonel Yorke though made an exception on this occasion and the location was permitted to open for passengers with a 8 inch overhang instead. Assuming the view was indeed taken around the date stated, then the fact a motor train is being used is interesting. The official opening notice referring to a service of 'Rail Motor Cars'. Does this mean a motor train was another name for these, or was it simply that this was the one service operated by a locomotive and trailer?

Lens of Sutton

RADFORD & TIMSBURY HALT

Situated between Paulton Halt and Camerton. Single timber platform 150ft. long with pagoda shelter authorised on 1 February 1906. The estimated cost of £625 included the cost of the Halt at Combe Hay. Opened on 9 May 1910 although temporarily closed from 22 March 1915 until 9 July 1923. Permanent closure from 21 September 1925.

further reading: *The Camerton Branch*. Pub. Wild Swan.

RADIPOLE HALT

150ft. timber platforms on both up and down lines between Upwey Junction and Weymouth. Pagoda shelters provided and opened on 1 July 1905. Access to the stopping place was from nearby Spa Road and illumination was by gas. Platforms replaced by concrete in 1946.

further reading: *The Abbotsbury Branch*. Pub. Wild Swan and The Story of the Westbury to Weymouth Line. Pub. OPC.

RAGLAN ROAD CROSSING HALT

Single timber platform between Raglan and Llandenny on the Ross to Little Mill Junction line. Spear fencing was erected at one end of the site, with access via a level crossing at the north end. Authorised on 30 October 1930 at an estimated cost of £182, and opened on 24 November 1930 on the site of the original Raglan Road station which had closed on 1 January 1876.

further reading: The Ross, Monmouth and Pontypool Road Line. Pub. Oakwood Press.

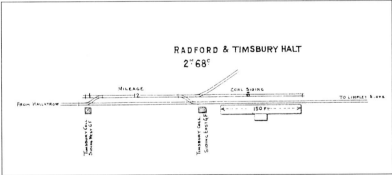

RADFORD & TIMSBURY HALT
2ᵐ 68ᶜ

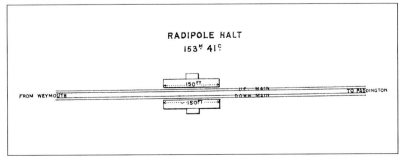

RADIPOLE HALT
153ᵐ 41ᶜ

Radipole Halt near Weymouth and viewed south, not long after opening. Unusually perhaps the up platform possessed access to either end, from the bridge behind the photographer, and seen clearly in the lower view, and also from the footpath on which the boy is standing. Aside from the name of the location, the running in board affords information as to which platform was required for trains in which direction. It is not clear if this was a common feature or unique to Radipole Halt. Certainly it was altered in later years to the conventional form seen below.

National Railway Museum / GWR 'C' series 55502

Radipole Halt again but this time in 1965 and viewed towards Dorchester. The location was now under the control of the Southern Region and although a number of original features still remain the original timber platform has at some stage been replaced by concrete. *H.F. Wheeller Collec. / Roger Carpenter*

RAILWAY TERRACE

Unadvertised stopping place with unknown facilities between St. Clear and South Caradon on the Liskeard and Caradon Railway. In use from about 1889 - 1896, and used mainly by excursion traffic, although it is alleged passengers may also have been carried on freight services.

RAVEN SQUARE

Situated on the narrow gauge Welshpool and Llanfair Light Railway between Seven Stars and Golfa. Closed 9 February 1921. Classified by the GWR as a 'Halt', although the suffix was not carried.

RED LION CROSSING HALT

Low height stone platform 212ft. * long on the single line Gwaun-cau-Gurwen branch between Garnant and Gwaun-cau-Gurwen, shelter provided. Authorised on 29 June 1905 and opened on 1 January 1908. Temporary closure from 2 April 1917 until 1 June 1920. Permanently closed from 4 May 1926 although officially reported in June 1928 as 'Not in use at present'.

Note: at the time the stopping place was authorised the intended platform size was given as 200ft. x 12ft.

REDWICH HALT

see entry for New Passage Halt

RESPRYN

Located between Bodmin Road and Lostwithiel. Formerly a public station but passed into private use from 27 June 1859 until at least August 1864. Facilities unknown.

RHEIDOL FALLS HALT

On the narrow gauge Vale of Rheidol branch between Aberffrwd and Rhiwfron. Ground level facilities opened on 7 March 1904 and trains called by request. Originally provided with a shelter although this was later reported as 'rusted away'. Closed in winter from 1 January 1931, and then fully from 31 August 1939. Seasonal re-opening from 23 July 1945. It is not known if the Halt suffix was carried. Receipts included with Devils Bridge.

further reading: *The Vale of Rheidol Light Railway.* Pub. Wild Swan.

RHIGOS HALT

Up and down platforms 200ft. long with shelters on the Vale of Neath line between Pontwalby Halt and Hirwaun Pond Halt. Authorised 26 May 1910 at an estimated cost of £635 to include the provision of paths. Opened on 1 May 1911.

RHIWBINA HALT

On the Cardiff Railway system between Whitchurch and Birchgrove Halt. Opened on 1 March 1911 with up and down platforms 50ft. long and believed possibly using the original spelling of 'Rhubina' - it is not clear if at this time the suffix was carried. At an unreported date authorisation was given for the platforms to be extended to 120ft. and then on 7 October 1926 to 200ft., the cost of which was an unspecified portion of £941 which included work elsewhere on the GWR system. However the accuracy of this latter work must be in doubt as on 30 May 1935 further extensions were authorised to 400ft. on each side and with the existing facilities reported as then being on the up side 271ft. and 199ft. on the down. An additional name board and lighting was also to be provided. The cost of the 1935 work was stated at £380. Supervision was exercised from Whitchurch.

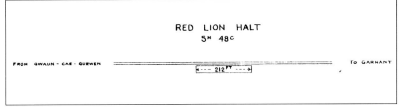

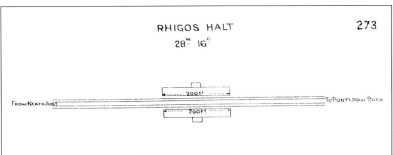

Rhigos Halt probably soon after opening and possibly slightly unusual in that solid platforms were provided even from an early period.

RHIWFRON HALT

Situated on the narrow gauge Vale of Rheidol line between Rheidol Falls Halt and Devils Bridge. Ground level platform and shelter provided from an unknown date but certainly prior to July 1904. Closed in winter from 1 January 1931 but reported as re-opened in summer from 23 July 1945 - possibly a similar closure occurred in 1939 as per Rheidol Falls Halt. It is not known if the suffix was carried. A siding was provided nearby to serve an extensive lode mine. Receipts included with Devils Bridge.

further reading: *The Vale of Rheidol Light Railway*. Pub. Wild Swan.

RHOS

Formerly a public station between Legacy and Brook Street Halt, and which from 1 January 1931 became an unadvertised stopping place used for excursion traffic.

RHOSROBIN HALT

Authorised on 23 June 1932 with staggered up and down platforms, footpaths and steps to the public road. Located between Wrexham General and Gresford and opened on 1 September 1932, closed 6 October 1947. The estimated cost of the stopping place was £257 plus refixing the shelters from the closed Moss Halt and Lodge Halt - respectively £33 and £30. Originally to have been called 'Pandy Bridge Halt.'

RHOS-Y-METRE HALT

Located between Cefn and Ruabon on the Didcot to Chester line. Authorised on 18 July 1906 at an estimated cost of £336. Opened on 1 September 1906 with 150ft. Up and down platforms of timber construction and with a shelter only on the down side. Tickets were issued and collected by the guard of trains whilst the lamps were trimmed and lit by the Whitehurst lad porter and extinguished by the guard of the last train.

RHYDYFELIN HALT

Up and down rail level platforms on the former Alexander Docks Railway, Caerphilly and Pontypridd line between Treforest Halt and Dynea Halt. Opened on 1 September 1904 and renamed High Level from 1 July 1924. On 14 May 1928 the stopping place was closed but replaced on the same day with another carrying the same name 18 chains east of the original site. The replacement work consisted of two standard height platforms with pagoda huts, the cost of the new works at this time was put at £230 plus a further £54 for extra foundations work caused due to meeting rock during the construction. This new work had been authorised on 26 January 1928. The name High Level; continued to be carried in the public timetables until at least 1939 - this despite the Low Level Halt having been closed in 1931. - see next entry.

Above: Rhydyfelin Halt on the Caerphilly and Pontypridd line, another of the ground level stopping places so typical of the lines in South Wales.

Rhydyfelin Halt on the former Cardiff Railway and by now the terminus of the line from Treforest. The somersault signals display their origins to the former owning company whilst the water tank was provided for the benefit of engines running round before returning.

RHYDYFELIN HALT

Situated on the former Cardiff Railway system between Treforest Low Level and Upper Boat. Up and down rail level platforms provided and opened on 1 March 1911. Renamed by the GWR Low Level from 1 July 1924 and closed 20 July 1931. From 1925 until closure the location served as the terminus of the line from Penrhos Junction and accordingly on 7 October 1926 provision of an additional 200ft. platform was authorised on the up side with shelter and approach road together with a new cross-over road and stop block. The line had been singled from 16 May 1928. On this date the standard height platform on the former up line came into use. See also Nantgarw Halt Low Level, where a platform was provided for the first time from this date. It is also significant that the High level Halt received standard height replacement platforms at this time.

Note: GWR Engineering Committee records report that on 29 January 1925 'improved accommodation' was authorised at Rhydyfelin Halt for £104. Presumably this was the Low Level site although the official source is not clear on this point.

RHYDYFELIN HALT HIGH LEVEL

see Rhydyfelin Halt, Alexander Docks Railway.

RHYDYFELIN HALT LOW LEVEL

see Rhydyfelin Halt, Cardiff Railway.

RIFLE RANGE HALT

Situated between Bewdley and Foley Park Halt. Single 106ft. platform with shelter on the east side of the line opened in June 1905 and closed on 4 October 1920 although retained in use albeit unadvertised 'for firing parties' until sometime after 1930. In June 1928 official records refer to the location as 'Not in use at present'.

ROBERTSTOWN HALT

see entry for Robertstown Platform

ROBERTSTOWN PLATFORM

Single platform on the Ynysybwl branch between Ynysybwl and Ynysybwl New Road Halt. Opened 1 November 1904, and renamed Robertstown Halt from 2 October 1922. Supervision exercised from Ynysybwl.

RODMARTON PLATFORM

This was the very first 'Platform' on the GWR and was opened on 1 September 1904. Located on the Tetbury branch between Jackaments Bridge Halt and Culkerton, facilities consisted a single platform 150ft. long with pagoda and access via steps to an un-metalled road passing under railway. The stopping place was on the south side of the railway. (Appropriately the Tetbury branch later witnessed some of the last wayside halts opened by BR in a vain attempt to stimulate traffic on rural branch lines.) Until 1905 the Platform suffix did not appear in the public timetable. Receipts included with Tetbury.

further reading: *The Tetbury Branch*. Pub. Wild Swan.

ROLLRIGHT HALT

Situated between Hook Norton and Chipping Norton on the Banbury and Cheltenham line. Single timber platform 151ft. long with corrugated pagoda and with access from a pathway leading up from the public road which passed under the railway. Opened on 12 December 1906 and lit by four oil lamps. Parcels traffic also handled.

further reading: *The Banbury & Cheltenham Railway*. Pub. OPC.

ROSE HEYWOOD

Unadvertised miners' stopping place between Abertillery and Blaina. Brought into use by July 1897 and closed sometime after 1918.

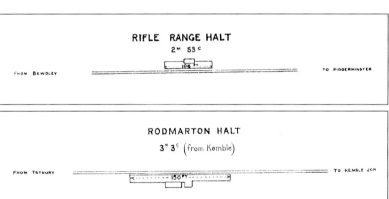

Rodmarton Halt, as it was then known, on the Tetbury branch, this ground level view looking towards Kemble. Access to the stopping place was by means of set of steps leading down to a minor road and which passed under the railway at the far end of the platform. The change of title from the original 'Platform' occurred at an unknown time and is another example of the confusion that existed over designations.

An undated and delightfully rural view of the Halt at Rollright - referred to locally as Great Rollright although this was never displayed on the name-board. Ironically though some 350 yards. east of the stopping place was a goods loop siding and which was officially referred to as Great Rollright Siding.

GREAT. ROLLRIGHT - YHE

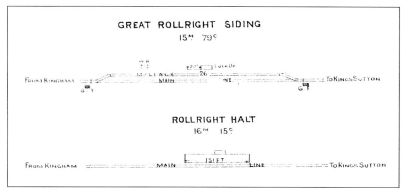

Rushwick Halt, a definite main line location , although the state of the track under the bridge would appear perhaps to be open to question!

ROWTON HALT

Situated between Crudginton and Ellerdine Halt on the Wellington to Crewe line. Authorised on 30 May 1935 with up and down platforms 80ft. long, shelters, name and notice boards and steps to the road. Estimated cost of construction £272. Opened 29 June 1935.

ROYAL AGRICULTURAL SHOW GROUND WARWICK

Situated on a spur from Cape Yard, Warwick and in use for showground traffic for a short time in May 1892. A similar facility was available for a brief period from July 1931 and at this later time possibly under the name 'Warwick Cape Yard'.

ROYAL WELSH AGRICUL-TURAL SHOW STATION

see entry in Appendix 1: Addendum to Volume 1 for Llanstephen Crossing.

RUBERY

Formerly a public station between Hunnington and Longbridge on the Longbridge and Halesowen joint line. Unadvertised, and used by workmen from April 1919 until about September 1936.

RUDDLE ROAD HALT

Staggered up and down platforms between Newnham and Awre Junction on the original South Wales main line, but never used by main line services. Opened 3

August 1907 in connection with the Newnham to Steam Mills Crossing rail motor service which started that day although as early as 1908 the shelter from one of the platforms was removed to the nearby Bullo Cross Halt. Ruddle Road Halt was closed on 30 April 1917 and the facilities removed on 30 June 1920.

RUNNEMEDE HALT.

see Runnemede Range.

RUNNEMEDE RANGE

Single platform on the Staines branch between Poyle Halt and Staines West. Originally an unadvertised stopping place which opened in mid-1897 it was advertised in the public timetables from 1 April 1892 possibly at that time with the name Runnemede Range Halt. Renamed Runnemede Halt in May 1934 although this did not appear in public timetables until 9 July 1934. Finally and from 4 November 1935 the location became known as Yeoveney Halt. The halt suffix was never used in timetables or on the nameboard.

RUNNEMEDE RANGE HALT

see Runnemede Range

RUSHWICK HALT

On the Worcester and Hereford line between Bransford Road and Boughton Halt. Up and down platforms opened on 31 March 1924.

RUSPIDGE HALT

Located on the Forest of Dean Central Branch between Bilson Halt and Staple Edge Halt. Single 125ft. long masonry platform with stone booking office and public access via a level crossing at the south end of the site. Opened on 3 August 1907, and from the outset both goods and parcels traffic were handled.

further reading: *The Forest of Dean Branch* Vol.1. Pub. Wild Swan.

Ruspidge Halt in the Forest of Dean and although classified as a halt by the GWR this was in reality a station. The view displays on the end of the building one of the seemingly rarely photographed notice boards displaying the words 'Rail Motor Cars' and followed by the train times.

The former station at St. Blazey and which was downgraded to 'Halt' status very early on. Despite the obvious facilities the station closed to passengers in 1925 although passenger trains from Par to Fowey and which of necessity reversed at St. Blazey, continued until 1929. Thereafter it was in use under 'Halt' status until 1934. The view was no doubt taken from the signal box and is looking towards Newquay.

This revision in status from station to halt status was by no means uncommon under the GWR and as is recounted in the main listings within the text, was the fate of a number of locations where traffic patterns no longer warranted the continuation of facilities. Later still under British Railways the practice would become far more common, cost cutting and line closures meaning major locations became in effect unstaffed halts for the final months of their lives. Accordingly this last category of BR halt is not included in this work, and simply because they were not regarded as such under the GWR .

Lens of Sutton.

Limited patronage awaiting No. 5557 arriving at St. Keyne with the 5.50 p.m. Liskeard to Looe, on 17 September 1957.

ST. ANDREWS ROAD PLATFORM

Workmen's platform situated between Avonmouth Dock and Hallen Marsh Junction. Provided with up and down platforms and reported as first used on 1 March 1917. Closed from 13 November 1922 but re-opened again this time as a public station with the name St. Andrews Road from 30 June 1924.

further reading: *Bristol Railway Panorama*. Pub. Millstream.

ST. ATHAN HALT

Between Gilestown and Llantwit Major. Authorised on 27 April 1939 with slightly staggered up and down platforms, shelters, booking office, name and notice boards, fencing, gates and lighting. Including the excavation for the platforms, the estimated cost was £1,272 although this was exceeded by a further £455 due to more rock being needed to be excavated than had been allowed for. Opened to the public from 1 September 1939 and re-classified as a station, minus the suffix from 3 May 1943

ST. BLAZEY

Formerly a public station situated between Par and Luxulyan. Used by workmen between 21 September 1925 and 29 December 1934. Up and down platforms provided.

further reading: *A Historical Survey of Great Western Stations Vol. 4* and *The Newquay Branch*. Both Pub. OPC.

ST. BUDEAUX PLATFORM

Located between Keyham and Saltash and opened on 1 June 1904. In the Engineers Minutes for 3 January 1906 there is an entry authorising, '...widening and lengthening of the platform to 400ft......provision of new booking office and waiting room on up side, erection of alcove on down side brought from Ford. Estimated cost of £445.'

ST. GERMANS VIADUCT

Temporary stopping place used by workmen between 1905 and approximately November 1915 during construction of the deviation line at this point. Located between Wiveliscombe and St. Germans.

ST. HARMONS

Between Pantydwr and Rhyader on the Moat Lane to Three Cocks Junction line. Formerly a full station, but downgraded on 2

Referred to as St. Keyne for St. Keyne Well on the nameboard this was nevertheless an official GWR Halt . The remains behind and beyond the platform were a former lime kiln but it is not clear if this had ever afforded any traffic to the railway. The view is looking towards Looe and which was just over three miles distant.

Roger Carpenter.

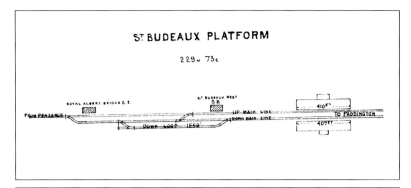

	No. of staff	Paybill £	Tickets Issued	Season Tickets	Parcels number	Total Receipts £
1913	4	299	1967	?	1664	1967
1923	4	784	3419	759	1764	3419
1929	4	506	2821	356	2297	2821
1930	4	608	2781	340	2419	2781
1931	4	583	2465	322	2509	2465
1932	4	581	2603	377	2568	2603
1933	4	634	2765	456	3903	2765
1934	4	637	3274	838	4810	3274
1936	4	658	3479	950	5489	3479
1936	4	667	3845	1070	7367	3845
1937	4	610	4744	1291	13241	4744
1938	5	727	5476	1436	17803	5476

Above: Traffic statistics for St. Budeaux Platform near Plymouth. As can be readily gleaned, the revenue gained from this location was considerable both in regard to passengers numbers and also with parcels and other 'smalls'. The LSWR and later the Southern Railway had their own stopping place with similar name on their own adjacent route and which resulted by 1947 in the GWR location being referred to as St. Budeaux (Ferry Road) with the SR stopping place given the suffix, Victoria Road.

Right:
Traffic statistics as are available for Saltney Halt. The records state that staff numbers and costs were included with that of Saltney Yard. The figures for 1932 were for a part year only as the location had opened on an unreported date in July.

	Tickets Issued	Season Tickets	Parcels number	Total Receipts £
1932	4177	26	1594	372
1933	7833	53	4681	900
1934	7512	56	6288	984
1935	8374	70	7065	806
1936	7307	62	7634	730
1937	6678	63	7584	781
1938	6283	93	7809	73

March 1936 although this was not shown in the public timetable nor on nameboards or on tickets.

ST. HILARY PLATFORM.

On the Taff Vale system between St. Mary Church and Cowbridge. Single platform opened 1 May 1906 and closed 12 July 1920. Reported in 1928 as 'not in use at present'. Facilities consisted a 40ft. platform with no shelter, intending passengers being confined to a pen at the rear of the platform and were then released to join the train by the guard. Apparently this was standard practice at the time at all rail level halts on all of the South Wales companies' lines.

further reading: *The Cowbridge Railway.* Pub. OPC.

ST. KEYNE

Single platform between Coombe Junction and Causeland. Opened 1 September 1902. It is not believed the 'Halt' suffix was ever carried.

further reading: *The Liskeard and Looe Branch.* Pub. Wild Swan.

ST. LAWRENCE PLATFORM

On the Boscarne Extension branch between Bodmin General and Wadebridge. Single platform opened 26 October 1906 and unstaffed. Incorrectly shown in 'Bradshaw' as a Halt and whilst referred to in the GWR Halt's register as a Platform in the official schematic drawings register it is captioned as a Halt! Closed 1 January 1917.

ST. MARY'S CROSSING HALT

Between Chalford and Brimscombe. Opened 12 October 1903. Up and down platforms provided. As the date would suggest this was one of the earliest 'halts' on the GWR system although it is not clear if the facilities were originally at ground level.

ST Y-NYLL PLATFORM

This page:

St. Mary's Crossing Halt between Chalford and Brinscombe and one of the first new stopping places in the Golden Valley, this one opened in October 1903. The photographs depict the location possibly after some form of rebuilding as it may well have been that at first it was a ground level stopping place. Official records are no help and give no reference to additional work in the form of platforms being provided. (Although it is not clear from the photographs, there were two platforms opposite each other.) One unusual feature apparent from the lower view, and which was recorded as having been taken in 1922, is the means of access to the platform, the steps at the end of the platform not a common feature. The roof of the shelter is also slightly different to that more commonly seen and could well have been one of several variations used by the GWR in the early days until a standard style was established. The Signal Box visible was at the west end of the site.

Credit: Lower - L.G.R.P. 8858

Cregiau and Penrhos Junction. Up and down platforms opened 1 May 1905, although it ceased to appear in the timetables from as early as 18 November 1905.

SALTNEY HALT

Between Balderton and Chester. Authorised on 17 March 1932 at an estimated cost of £470. Facilities included up and down platforms, booking and parcels office on the down side, name boards, fencing, gates and lighting. A note in the records states, '...the shelters used at this location were recovered from Chirk.' There was also an extensive yard facility at Saltney, which had existed for some years prior to 1932. An oblique reference in the GWR Traffic Statistics reveals an entry for passenger returns for 'Saltney Passenger' for the years 1903 and 1913. This was the original Saltney & Chester station which closed on 1 January 1917. The halt possibly utilised the old platforms. The halt suffix did not appear in timetables although it did on tickets.

SAMPFORD PEVERELL HALT

Authorised on 24 April 1928 and located between Burlescombe and Tiverton Junction. The original, slightly staggered facilities consisted, a down platform 400ft. long and an up island platform 500ft. long. Both these were of timber construction and an alcove and lock up were also provided. Opening took place on 9 July 1928, with an estimated £2,568 having been spent. In the early part of 1933 and in connection with the quadrupling of the main line at this point, new up and down running loops were provided and accordingly the platforms were resited and rebuilt facing the loops. Masonry was used for the new works at this time.

further reading: *A Historical Survey of Great Western Stations Vol. 4.* Pub. OPC.

SANDPLACE

Single platform between Causeland and Looe. Opened in 1881. 'Halt' suffix not displayed.

further reading: *The Liskeard and Looe Branc'.* Pub. Wild Swan.

SANDSFOOT CASTLE HALT

Single platform between Rodwell and Wyke Regis. Opened 1 August 1932. On 29 April 1937 authorisation was given for the provision of a footbridge at an estimate of £465, the cost equally divided with the Southern Railway.

further reading: *The Isle of Portland Railway. Vol. 2.* Pub. Oakwood Press.

SARSDEN HALT

Located between Kingham and Chipping Norton. Between July 1897 and 2 July 1906 was in use only as a private stopping place for an unknown purpose but using the name 'Sarsden Siding'. Passenger facilities at this time are likewise unknown. From July 1906, a standard height platform was provided with a corrugated waiting room and parcels traffic was also handled. Intended to serve the village of Churchill, it might be reasonable to expect the stopping place to carry this name. However, Earl Ducie who lived at Sarsden House beyond the village requested the alternative be used.

Sandplace on the Liskeard & Looe Railway and photographed in 1909. GWR 4-4-0ST No. 13 at the time on hire to the line and arriving at a well patronised stopping place. The light track will be noted.

Roger Carpenter

further reading: *The Banbury & Cheltenham Railway*. Pub. OPC.

SARSDEN SIDING

see entry for Sarsden Halt.

SCAFELL CUTTING

Private stopping place between Newtown and Moat Lane Junction. In use by 1873 although the designation 'Cutting' was dropped by May 1876. Closed 1 July 1891 but re-opened around July 1913. It was advertised in timetables only by means of a footnote and referred to as Scafell halt at least until 1924. By 1935 it had become Scafell. Goods traffic was handled although this ceased from March 1941. The facilities are known to have been available for the up line only.

SCAFELL HALT

see entry for Scafell.

SEBASTAPOL HALT

Between Panteg & Griffithstown and Pontrhydyrun on the Hereford, Blaenavon and Newport line. Authorised on 6 October 1927 with paths, steps to public road, gates and booking office. Estimated cost of £1,366. Opened in June 1928 and originally staffed. It became unstaffed from April 1933, although a porter was re-instated again from 24 July 1935. Facilities included round top corrugated iron shelters. No Halt or other suffix

The Guard issuing tickets at Sandplace in September 1953.

John Bourne

was displayed on nameboards, tickets or in timetables. The name of the location was taken from a group of nearby houses built at the time of the Crimean War and in common with other areas in South Wales. Parcels traffic was also handled.

SEER GREEN HALT

see entry for Beaconsfield Golf Links Halt. Raised to station status by 1935.

SEMINGTON HALT

Between Seend and Holt Junction. Single platform opened either 3 August or 1 October 1906 and with parcels traffic handled by anagent

from 1 February 1909.

further reading: *GWR to Devizes*. Pub. Millstream.

SERRIDGE PLATFORM

On the Severn & Wye system between Speech House Road and Drybrook Road. Opened in 1878 with a single platform provided, which ceased to appear in timetables from October 1879. Only down trains called, by request, because of the stiff gradient facing up trains at this point.

further reading: *The Severn & Wye Railway Vol. 2*. Pub. Wild Swan.

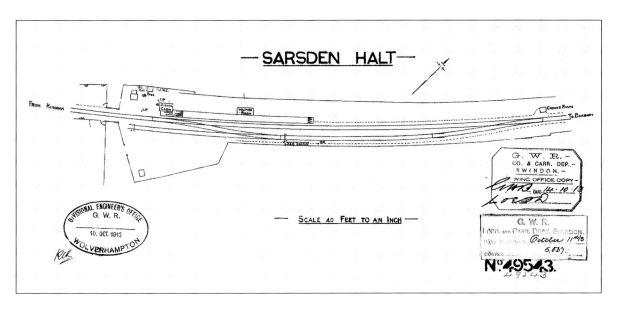

SARSDEN HALT.

Sarsden Halt on the Banbury to Cheltenham Line and portrayed probably soon after completion in 1906. The signal box was ostensibly provided due to the level crossing but also served to control the points leading from the goods siding at what was the Kingham end of the site. Notice the post supporting the lamp and which appears to be a continuation of the fence post. The track is all of the inside keyed variety whilst there is also a good view of the point disc. This wonderful photograph was discovered in a box of odd items in a junk shop and purchased for just a few pence. It would be fascinating to see nos. 1-23 as well!

Sarsden Halt again but this time with a '517' class 0-4-2T paused at the platform with a train of what appear to be crimson liveried 4-wheel vehicles. No doubt typical also of services on the line in the early days of the 20th. century.

Below:
Semington Halt north of Devizes in 1952. The non standard height platform was provided in 1909 and was never raised to conventional height.
L.G.R.P. 26262

SESSWICK HALT

Single platform between Pickhill Halt and Marchweil. First appeared in timetables from October 1913. A £150 extension of the platform was authorised on 25 April 1940, although records then show the stopping place as being closed from 10 June 1940. Re-opening took place on 6 May 1946.

SEVERN BEACH

Referred to in an undated GWR document as 'Severn Beach Platform', and opened on 5 June 1922 on the Avonmouth and Pilning line. Excursion trains ran on 5 and 6 June 1922, being the Whit Monday and Tuesday holidays. For the remainder of June and the first week of July trains ran only on Wednesdays and Sundays. It acquired station status and a daily service from 10 July 1922.

further reading: *Bristol Railway Panorama*. Pub. Millstream and Lines to Avonmouth. Pub. OPC.

SEVERN BEACH PLATFORM

see entry for Severn Beach.

SHAUGH BRIDGE PLATFORM

On a curve between Bickleigh and Clearbrook Halt. Single timber platform and corrugated shelter opened either 19/21 August or 19 October 1907. At a later time the platform was replaced by a masonry structure. The stopping place was especially popular with trippers on summer weekends, and at this time was staffed from Bickleigh by a porter or porter/signalman. It is said that prior to 1939 there were even some Tea Rooms at the location, which then would probably make the location unique - in reality these were no doubt outside the boundary fence and privately owned. Access was via a short path from the nearby road.

further reading: *The Tavistock, Launceston and Princetown Railways*. Pub. Oakwood Press.

SHIPTON-ON-CHERWELL HALT

Between Kidlington and Blenheim & Woodstock. Single platform with open timber staging and small lean-to shelter provided. Opened 1 April 1929, with receipts included with Blenheim & Woodstock.

further reading: *The Woodstock Branch*. Pub. Wild Swan.

SHUT END HALT

It is believed this was a 1925 proposal for a stopping place on the Kingswinford branch between Gornal and Pensford at the time this route was being widened and adapted for passenger traffic. Facilities were to have been up and down platforms 250ft. long with shelters and steps to road. Also a footbridge over a loop on the down side. None of this was ever built.

further reading: *The Railway to Wombourn*. Pub. Uralia Press.

SILIAN HALT

Between Lampeter and Blaenplwyf Halt. Single platform opened 12 May 1911. Traffic receipts from this location were limited in the extreme. Just £25 revenue in 1913 and corresponding to 54 tickets of which only £4 originated from the halt itself. Matters were little improved by 1923 and although there was a sudden peak at £1159 in 1929, the figure had dropped again to £123 the following year and £14 by 1934. The last year for which figures are available, 1936, revealed £187 of revenue.

SIX BELLS HALT

Between Aberbeeg and Abertillery. Authorised on 27 June 1935 at an estimated cost of £4,715. Facilities included an island platform 250ft. long, footpath approach, shelter, booking office, name and notice boards, w/c, and lighting. Also a footbridge to connect the platform with the approaches and a new dry wall and extension of the existing retaining walls. Opened on 27 September 1937. On 30 May 1946 additional facilities in the form of improved lavatory accommodation was approved for £369. Another halt carrying the same name was located on the former LNWR rynmawr to Abersychan & Talywaun line, but this became Garndiffaith Halt from 2 October 1922.

Sesswick Halt between Pickhill Halt and Marchweil. The view is one of those clearly attributable to the late John Smith of Lens of Sutton and who in the 1950's and 60's would travel hundreds of miles by cycle recording the stations and halts of the contemporary railway scene. One of his trademarks being to chalk the name of the site on a board facing the camera.
Lens of Sutton

SHAUGH HALT.

Shaugh Bridge Platform in its delightful moor land setting and easy to see why the location was so popular with trippers. The top view could well be taken during the Edwardian era although even at this early stage the confusion in names is apparent with the 'Halt' designation used by the photographer. In later years there was equal confusion, with the suffix appearing at the south end of the stopping place - centre photograph, but not at the north end - lower view. The locomotive at the head of the 4.52 p.m. Tavistock to Plymouth train, was recorded as No. 3629 and the photograph taken on 16 September 1957.

SHAUGH BRIDGE

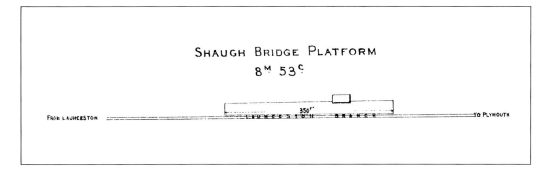

SHAUGH BRIDGE PLATFORM
8ᴹ 53ᶜ

FROM LAUNCESTON   350ᶠᵗ   LAUNCESTON BRANCH   TO PLYMOUTH

Shipton-on-Cherwell on the Woodstock branch and the only intermediate stopping place on the line. Access was from a 'kissing-gate' alongside the Banbury Road.   *Both: R.C. Riley*

Slough Trading Estate platform shown here devoid of passengers but with an unidentified '2-6-2T' lurking on the extreme left platform. Considerable rail traffic originated from this location for may years and with passenger services served by a shuttle from the main station.

Lens of Sutton

South Greenford Halt and depicted in 1968. Sometime between 1957 and the above date the original timber platforms had been replaced whilst in more recent times the pagoda shelters have been superseded by 'bus stop' type units.

David Hyde.

SLOUGH DEPOT

see entry for Slough Trading Estate.

SLOUGH TRADING ESTATE

Private stopping place having four platform faces on the expansive Slough Trading Estates system from Slough station. Into use from 17 March 1919 and renamed Slough Depot by 24 September 1928.

further reading: *The Slough Estates Railway.* Pub. Wild Swan.

SNATCHWOOD HALT

Between Pontnewyd and Abersychan Low Level. Authorised on 9 June 1910 with staggered 150ft. platforms, shelters 20ft. x 7ft. and paths, the estimated cost of which was £377. Opened on 13 July 1912. Note: the first known plan for this location is dated as early as 19 March 1908, some two years before formal authorisation was given.

SOUTH AYLESBURY HALT

Single platform between Little Kimble and Aylesbury on the Great Western / Great Central joint line. Opened 13 February 1933, with receipts included with Aylesbury.

SOUTH GREENFORD HALT

Between Castle Bar Halt and Greenford. Up and down platforms lit by paraffin vapour lighting and opened on 20 September 1926, receipts included with either Southall or Greenford. On 29 April 1937, electric lighting was authorised together with alterations to the ramps for an estimated cost of £154. Then on 27 July 1939, an extension of the platforms was approved for a further £170.

SOUTH HAREFIELD HALT

see entry for Harefield Halt.

SOUTH MARSTON FACTORY PLATFORM

Located on a short branch line off the Highworth branch from Stratton and used by workmen between 5

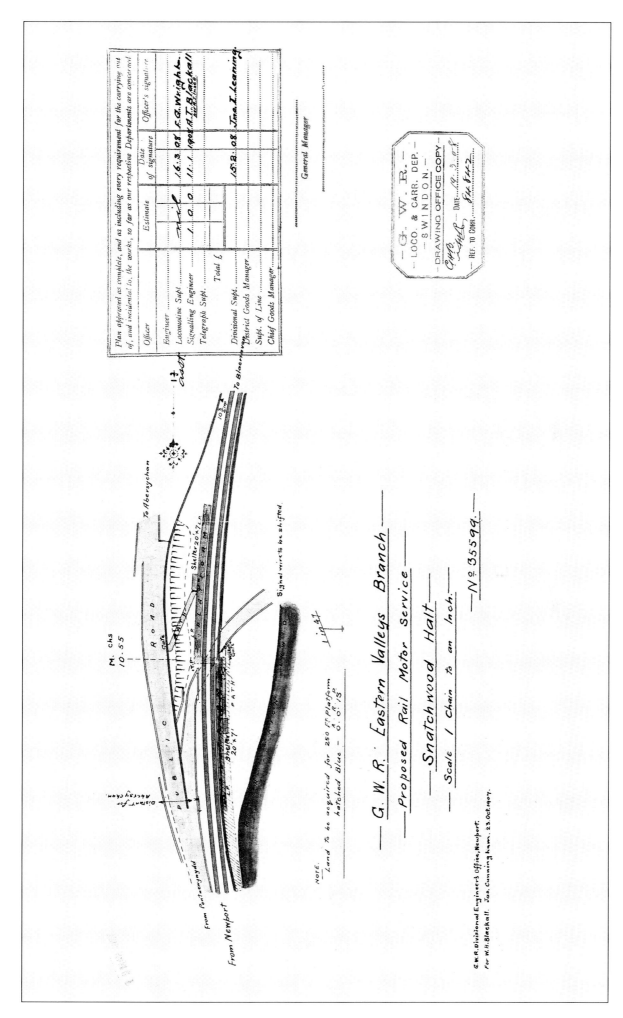

G.W.R. Eastern Valleys Branch

Proposed Rail Motor Service

Snatchwood Halt

Scale 1 Chain to an Inch.

No. 35599.

June 1941 and an unreported date in 1944. (The location was also later re-opened for a brief period under British Railways.) Facilities consisted of a single masonry platform with booking office, waiting room and run-round loop.

further reading: *The Highworth Branch*. Pub. Wild Swan.

SOUTH PIT HALT

see entry for Glyncorrwg / Glyncorrwg Colliery.

SPEEN

Single platform on the west side of the Lambourn Valley branch between Newbury West Fields Halt and Stockcross & Bagnor. Originally provided with a 120ft. x 9ft. x 9ins. platform this was raised to standard height by the GWR in the period 1907-9 and also increased in size to 169ft. x 12ft. plus ramps. From this time also a corrugated shelter and wooden ticket office were also provided. Staffing was in the hands of a porter / gatekeeper. Although officially designated a Halt by the GWR, the suffix was not carried.

further reading: *The Lambourn Branch*. Pub. Wild Swan.

SPRING ROAD HALT

see entry for Spring Road Platform.

SPRING ROAD PLATFORM

Between Tyseley and Hall Green. Up and down platforms opened 1 July 1908. A note in the records refers to,"...refixing corrugated hut removed from Wooten Wawen Halt at a cost of £170." No date for this is given. By 2 February 1922, the stopping place is referred to as Spring Road Halt and with the suffix dropped completely from 7 July 1924 although it is not certain if this corresponds with an official upgrade to station status at this time. Parcels traffic was handled. On 22 March 1928 an extension of both platforms by 100ft. to cater for '...increased passenger traffic...' was authorised together with additional lighting and the necessary removing and refixing of the platform ramps. The estimated cost of the work being £290.

STANLEY BRIDGE HALT

Between Chippenham and Black Dog Halt on the Calne branch. Single platform opened on 3 April 1905, and originally provided with a corrugated pagoda and timber milk shed although this feature was removed in later years. Parcels traffic handled by an agent from 1 February 1909, and supervision exercised from Chippenham.

further reading: *The Calne Branch*. Pub. Wild Swan.

Speen on the Lambourn Valley line and with a Newbury train entering on 9 April 1959. On the platform is Mrs. Edith McCartney the resident porter and who aside from being responsible for the issue and collection of tickets would also deliver parcels in the local area courtesy of the railway cycle. With one exception and despite designated as such, none of the intermediate stopping places on the Lambourn line displayed the 'Halt' suffix.

E.T. Gill

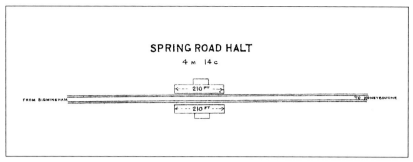

SPRING ROAD HALT
4 m 14 c

FROM BIRMINGHAM ← -- 210 FT --→ TO HONEYBOURNE
← -- 210 FT --→

STANLEY BRIDGE HALT.
2 M 4 C

FROM CALNE ← -- 149 FT -- → TO CHIPPENHAM

Stanley Bridge Halte - note the spelling, circa 1910, and a good example of how even such a small location played its part in both serving the community and affording revenue to the railway. There are for example a number of churns, either awaiting loading or possible collection by the farmers.

Stanley Bridge Halt in its final days. The original name board survives but with the wording moved whilst the milk producer is still present even though the finished product no longer travels by train.

Paul Strong

Staverton Halt on what was then the important route from Trowbridge (Bradford Junction) to Chippenham via Melksham. Dating as it did from 1905 it is perhaps slightly unusual that pagoda type shelters are not provided although there is no earlier view available to confirm if a change had perhaps taken place.

D. Thompson

STANNER

Between Kington and New Radnor. Former station which was downgraded on 28 July 1941.

STANWARDINE HALT

Between Baschurch and Haughton Halt. Up and down platforms opened 27 February 1933.

STANWELL MOOR & POYLE

see entry for Poyle Halt.

STAPLE EDGE HALT

Between Upper Soudley Halt and Ruspidge Halt. Single platform opened 3 August 1907.

further reading: *The Severn & Wye Railway Vol. 1.* Pub. Wild Swan.

STAVERTON HALT

Between Holt Junction and Bradford Junction. Up and down platforms opened 16 October 1905.

STEAM FERRY CROSSING HALT

see entry for Kingswear Level Crossing.

STEAM MILLS CROSSING HALT

Between Nailbridge and Whimsey Halt. Opened 3 August 1907 and closed 7 July 1930. Possibly the original facilities were at ground level, although later a wooden platform and pagoda were provided.

further reading: *A Historical Survey of Forest of Dean Railways,*

Track Layouts and Illustrations. Pub. OPC, and The Forest of Dean Branch Vol. 2. Pub. Wild Swan.

STOCKCROSS & BAGNOR

Between Speen and Boxford on the Lambourn Valley line. Originally with a low height platform, this was rebuilt in similar style to Speen. (see earlier entry). Only a corrugated iron pagoda was provided by the GWR. Unstaffed from 9 July 1934, at which time it was designated a Halt although the suffix was not carried.

further reading: *The Lambourn Branch.* Pub. Wild Swan.

STOCKTON CROSSING

Between Codford and Wylye. Used by workmen (and possibly the military) between 1907 and approximately July 1915.

STOKE PRIOR HALT

Between Steens Bridge and Leominster. Single platform opened 8 July 1929.

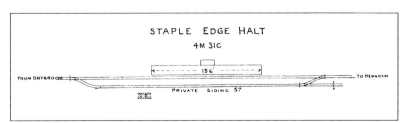

STAPLE EDGE HALT
4M 31C

FROM DRYBROOK   TO NEWNHAM
PRIVATE SIDING 57

STOTTESDON

On the former Cleobury Mortimer and Ditton Priors railway between Prescott and Aston Botterell siding. Opened 20 November 1908 and classified by the GWR as a Halt from 1 October 1923, although the suffix was not displayed. Facilities consisted of a low height platform, lamp hut and substantial timber waiting shed of typical CMDP design. Closed to passengers from 26 September 1938 and to goods from 11 September 1939.

further reading: *The Cleobury Mortimer & Ditton Priors Railway*. Pub. OPC.

STRAP LANE HALT

Up and down platforms between Witham and Bruton authorised on 26 May 1932, and consisting of shelters, name board, lighting, drainage, footpath, gates and steps to the public road. Estimated cost of £500. Opened on 18 July 1932. Temporary closure reported from 6 October 1941 to 12 June 1946 although Bradshaws for May 1942 still includes it.

further reading: *The Story of the Westbury to Weymouth Line*. Pub. OPC.

STRATFORD-ON-AVON EVESHAM ROAD CROSSING HALT

South of the main station on the line to Honeybourne and Cheltenham. 100ft. platforms opened 17 October 1904 and closed 14 July 1916.

further reading: *The Stratford on Avon to Cheltenham Railway*. Pub. Irwell Press.

STRATFORD-ON-AVON RACECOURSE PLATFORM

Located between Stratford-on-Avon and the site of Chambers Crossing Halt. Authorised on 27 April 1933 with up and down platforms 550ft. long, name board, ticket barriers, fencing, gates and

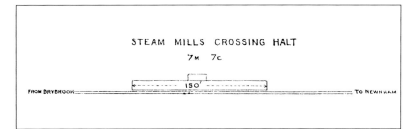

According to Ian Pope this is the only known view of Steam Mills Crossing Halt, visible to the right of the crossing and which served a small settlement at the bottom of Cinderford.   Lens of Sutton

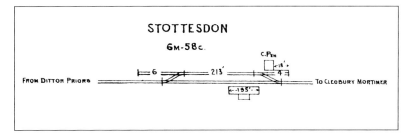

Stottesdon on the former independent Cleobury Mortimer & Ditton Priors Railway and viewed towards the terminus at Ditton Priors. The independent origins of the railway are apparent from the non-standard shelter whilst the location owes everything to Halt type status although line the Lambourn line the designation was not carried.

Roger Carpenter

'3582' leaving Strap Lane Halt on the Westbury -Taunton auto service sometime in 1935. After temporary closure from 1941 to 1946, it was finally closed permanently from 5 June 1950.

L.G.R.P. 626

Strap Lane Halt on the GWR main line to the west and which when it was opened in 1932 was one of 14 such wayside stopping places opened by the GWR in that year.

Stratton Park Halt. Despite its proximity to Swindon - just two miles east, records show that receipts for this location were small. Only three years figures are known of, in 1933 260 tickets were issued for a gross revenue of just £9, in 1934 1727 tickets for £64, and the following year, 1935, 450 tickets for £11. Any figures after this time were included with those from Swindon.

D.J. Hyde Collec.

lighting. Estimated cost of £823. Opened on 6 May 1933 and used for racecourse traffic only.

further reading: The Stratford on Avon to Cheltenham Railway. Pub. Irwell Press.

STRATTON PARK HALT

Between Shrivenham and Swindon. Up and down platforms opened on 20 November 1933, having been authorised on 23 March 1933 at an estimated cost of £457. Originally intended to have been called 'Stratton Green Halt'. Aside from the 150ft. x 8ft. platforms there were also shelters, footpaths and steps to the public road. Originally lit by oil kept in a specially provided oil hut, electric lighting was later installed for £459.

STRETTON WESTWOOD HALT / STRETTON WESTWOOD CROSSING HALT

Between Much Wenlock and Presthope. Believed either a private stopping place or unadvertised and thought to have been in use by 1933. Public use commenced on 7 December 1935 when it was renamed Westwood Halt.

SUN BANK HALT

see entry for Garth and Sun Bank Halt.

SUTTON VENY CAMP

Served by a branch from Heytesbury to a Military Hospital. In use between 1916 and 1925.

SWANBRIDGE HALT

Between Lavernock and Sullyon on the Taff Vale system. Up and down platforms provided for the opening in June 1906 and extended in 1917.

SWANSEA EAST DEPOT TICKET PLATFORM

Between Briton Ferry Road and Swansea Wind Street stations. Dates of use are unknown although it is known to have been used for ticket examination. In use by 1867, in which year it was also briefly advertised as an alighting point. Wind Street station was only open between 1 August 1863 and 1 March 1873 and which are therefore the 'extreme' dates for the use of this platform.

SWINDON 'G' BOX

In the vicinity of Swindon Station and used by railway workmen only between July 1897 and, at the latest

November 1915. May also have been known as 'Swindon 'G' Cabin'.

SWINDON 'G' CABIN

see entry for Swindon 'G' Box.

SWINDON WORKS

Between Swindon and Purton. Used by railwaymen from some time prior to 1880 until approximately July 1897.

(Swindon Works was also the departure point for many of the annual 'trip' specials to various destinations. These trains however commenced from within the works complex.)

SYLFAEN FARM SIDING

On the narrow gauge Welshpool & Llanfair railway between Golfa and Castle Caereinion. Opening date not reported but certainly before July 1904, known to have closed to passengers on 1 February 1913. Re-opened to passengers at an unreported date before July 1922 and this time carrying the name 'Sylfaen Halt'. Finally closed to both passengers and goods from 9 February 1931.

SYLFAEN HALT
see entry for Sylfaen Farm Siding.

Tackley Halt and dating from 1931. The view is looking towards Oxford and with the shelters yet another variation in design. The reason for this may well have been that local contractors were used and instructed to provide a suitable shelter, if necessary to their own design - possibly also if GWR stocks were perhaps not available at that time. Certainly recourse was made to the conventional corrugated pagoda at a number of locations opened in subsequent years. In view of the number of halts built by the GWR it is perhaps not altogether surprising that official views only survive for a representative selection., this being one of those where no early photograph has been located.

Teigl Halt on the line from Blaenau Festiniog through to Bala,. The short platform was on the east side of the line, whilst the sharp curves so typical of much of this route and rugged scenery are both accentuated well. The check rail will also be noted. It should perhaps be stated that the GWR was not the only user of the type of shelter seen her, there were also some on the SR in Cornwall at small stopping places although never of course so numerous as on GWR lines. Additionally the GWR used the design as additional accommodation at various stations. The structure a cheap means of providing this when necessary.

R.C. Riley

TACKLEY HALT

Located between Bletchington and Heyford. Authorised on 27 November 1930 at an estimated cost of £385, for up and down platforms, waiting shelters, lamp hut, nameboard, fencing, lighting and drainage. Opened 6 April 1931.

TAFF MERTHYR COLLIERY HALT

Unadvertised stopping place between Trelewis Platform and Bedlinog. Provided with up and down platforms of standard height although unusually one was of masonry and the other of timber. The masonry platform was surmounted by a lean-to brick shelter. In use by September 1928.

TALLEY ROAD

Formerly a station between Llandilo and Llangadock on the Central Wales line. It was downgraded on 2 June 1941.

TALSARN HALT

Single platform between Blaenplwyf Halt and Felin Fach and opened on 12 May 1911. Parcels traffic also handled. Originally to have been called 'Penwern' although it is not thought this was ever carried.

see also, *Great Western Journal. No. 16.* Pub. Wild Swan.

TALWRN BACH HALT

Between Dyffryn-on-Sea and Llanbedr & Pensarn. Single 101ft. platform provided with round-topped corrugated shelter and public access via a level crossing. Opened 9 July 1923. - see entry also for Tygwyn Halt.

further reading: *The Cambrian Coast Railway.* Pub. Foxline.

TALYBONT HALT

On the Cambrian system between Dyffryn on Sea and Llanabar Halt. Single platform provided with round top corrugated shelter and which first appeared in the public timetable in July 1914. Unstaffed and supervised from Barmouth.

further reading: *The Cambrian Coast Railway.* Pub. Foxline.

TEIGL HALT

Opened 14 September 1931, single platform provided, and located between Manod and Festiniog.

TEIGNGRACE HALT

Between Newton Abbot and Heathfield. Formerly a full station but downgraded to 'Halt' status sometime between 1928 and 8 May 1939. Single platform provided.

further reading: *The Moretonhampstead Branch.* Pub. Waterfront.

THE HAWTHORNS HALT

Originally consisted of a single platform on the Stourbridge branch between Handsworth Junction and Smethwick Junction, which opened as an unadvertised halt on 25 December 1931 to serve the West Bromwich Albion football ground. At an unreported date there is a reference to platforms on the up and down main lines at this point although it is not clear if these were the original features. Costs are likewise unclear but at some point £1,044 was spent on the location, and then it is known that in December 1932 £2,185 was spent which included a new footbridge and footpath.

THE LAKES HALT

Situated between Wood End and Earlswood Lakes and consisting up and down platforms which opened on Monday 3 June 1935.

The Lakes Halt, south towards Henley-in-Arden in February 1966. Under the GWR receipts were included with either Earlswood Lakes or Henley-in Arden stations.
Andrew Muckley

THE LODGE HALT

see entry for Lodge Halt. (Further information to hand reveals the location opened on 1 July 1906 and closed 1 January 1931.)

THORNEY & KINGSBURY HALT

Between Langport (West) and Martock. Single platform opened 28 November 1927 and originally intended to have been simply 'Kingsbury Halt'. On 28 April 1932, authorisation was given for a new siding for milk traffic.

THORNFORD BRIDGE HALT

Authorised on 28 November 1936

The single platform at Thorney & Kingsbury Halt and which utilised the space originally intended for a second line of rails. The milk siding referred to in the text can be seen in the background.

with staggered up and down platforms and located between Yeovil and Yetminster. Opened 23 March 1936 and provided with 150ft. platforms, steps and path to the public road, shelters, name and notice boards, gates, lamp hut and Tilley lamps. Estimated cost of £463.

further reading: *The Story of the Westbury to Weymouth Line.* Pub. OPC.

TILE MILL HALT

This was a proposal dated 13 March 1928 for a Halt between Theale and Aldermaston. No proceeded with.

Thornford Bridge Halt and which utilised steps from a dissecting road bridge to reach either platform. The halt was approximately one mile form the village of the same name.

TINKER'S GREEN HALT

Single platform between Oswestry and Whittington (High Level), and approved on 5 October 1939 at an estimated cost of £445. Opened 16 October 1939. Originally to have been called 'Tinkers Halt'. This halt served large army camps and was staffed. In consequence it also carried relatively large stocks of tickets, particularly Forces Leave and Duty tickets, many of which were printed to distant destinations. It also enjoyed a shuttle service from Oswestry and which was locally arranged but not widely advertised.

TINTERN QUARRY SIDING

Unadvertised stopping place between Netherhope Halt and Tintern on the Wye Valley branch. Opened sometime after February 1931 when the siding was provided and used by workmen at the quarry.

TIR CELYN PLATFORM

Unadvertised halt for private landowner between Aberedw and Erwood on the Moat Lane to Three Cocks Junction Line. May also have been spelt 'Tyr Celyn Platform'. Dates of use are not certain, although possibly as early as 1872.

further reading: *The Mid Wales Railway.* Pub. Oakwood Press.

TONFANAU HALT

This stopping place on the Cambrian system between Towyn and Llangelynin is described as a Halt by C.C. Green in his book, *The Coast Lines of the Cambrian Railway.* Pub. by Wild Swan. It does not appear to have carried the suffix.

TONLLWYD HALT

Single platform between Godreaman Halt and Black Lion Crossing Halt. Opened on 1 January 1906 and closed on 2 January 1922.

TONMAWR PLATFORM

Single platform situated on the Port Talbot Railway's line from Port Talbot to Cymmer and Corrwg Merthyr Colliery. In 1920 the colliery company arranged with the Port Talbot Railway to run one return trip per day from Port Talbot to Corrwg Merthyr and by 1921 80ft. long halts had been provided at Cwmavon, Efail Fach, Tonmawr and Corrwg Merthyr. The company was informed that, if the platform at Tonmawr were to be extended to 120ft., then not more than one public train per day could be run from Port Talbot. During November 1922 the public service started - but ran only on Saturdays! It would seem as though Tonmawr achieved station status at this time, being renamed Tonmawr Junction.

TONTEG HALT

see entry for Tonteg Platform.

TONTEG HALT

On the Cadoxton line between Treforest (High Level) and Efail Isaf. Opened on 5 May 1930 with staggered up and down platforms.

TONTEG HALT

On the Llantrisant branch between Tonteg Junction and Church Village Halt. Opened on 5 May 1930 with a single platform.

TONTEG PLATFORM

Between Treforest and Church Village on the Taff Vale system. First appeared in the public timetable in May 1905 and renamed Tonteg Halt in timetables commencing 1 October 1923. Closed on 5 May 1930 being replaced by a new stopping place with platforms on the diverted Llantrisant and Cadoxton lines.

TORYBANWEB COLLIERY HALT

see entry for Corrwg Merthyr Navigation Colliery Halt.

TOWERSEY HALT

Single platform with standard

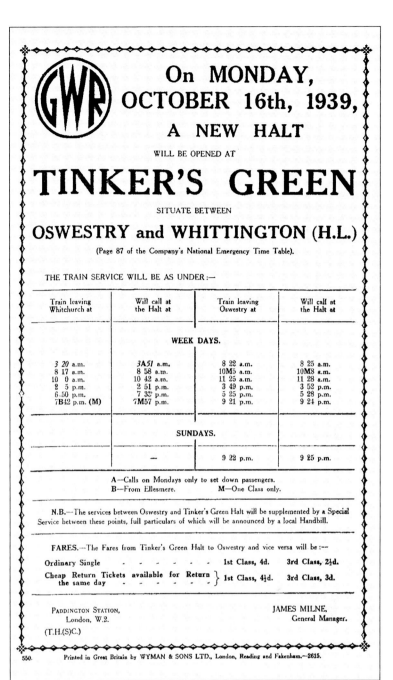

Tinker's Green Halt in peacetime days and viewed towards Whittington. Official records appertaining to this location are probably not exactly accurate and it is likely the formal approval of 5 October 1939 was retrospective, as it is unlikely the facilities could have been provided in just 11 days.

Towersey Halt and which dated from 5 June 1933. The path affording access led from the Towersey to Chinnor Road and was about ¹/₄ mile from the village of the same name. Construction was of 16 timber 'bays' plus ramps. As with Horspath Halt - see Volume , the high vantage point allowed the name to be displayed on both sides of the running in board as is displayed here to advantage.

Lens of Sutton

Before the advent of the private motor car and even with road bus competition, the halt could still be busy in the 1950's. This was the scene on 11 April 1955, with passengers waiting to board the 11.30 a.m. Oxford to Princess Risborough service.

Norman Simmons

corrugated pagoda shelter authorised on 26 March 1933 at an estimated cost of £210, and located between Thame and Bledlow. Opened on 5 June 1933 with receipts included with Thame. Public access to the stopping place by means of a cinder path leading up the embankment from road level.

further reading: *The Princess Risborough, Thame, Oxford Railway.* Pub OPC.

TRADING ESTATE

A single platform serving an industrial system off the Wrexham and Ellesmere line near Sesswick Halt.

TRAM ROAD HALT

see entry for Pontypridd Tram Road Halt.

TRAVELLERS REST (ABERCYNON UPPER)

Located between Nelson and Cilynydd. Single platform opened on 1 May 1901 and renamed 'Abercynon Upper' from 1 July 1924. Closed on 12 September 1932. It is questionable as to whether this was really a Halt. It was never so described in timetables, particularly Bradshaw, where other halts on this line are mentioned only in the usual footnote style. The platform was masonry and the building a substantial brick structure with canopy similar to that at Nelson and Cilfynydd. It was clearly staffed at least during Taff Vale Railway days, for the obligatory station bible (with the station name embossed into the leather cover) still exists.

TRAWSFYNYDD CAMP

Unadvertised stopping place near to Trawsfynydd station and serving a nearby army camp. In use from November 1911 for an unknown period. Facilities consisted two platforms, one 477ft. and the other 471ft. long. The latter narrowed for a distance of 200ft. to provide a

gun platform and end-on dock. In addition to a corrugated warehouse, lavatories and a guards room were provided.

further reading: *A Historical Survey of Great Western Stations, Layouts and Illustrations. Vol. 4.* Pub. OPC

TRAWSFYNYDD LAKE HALT

Single platform between Trawsfynydd and Maentrog Road opened on Saturday 14 April 1934.

TRECWN SIDINGS

Situated on the branch from Letterston Junction to serve a Naval Depot. In use by 1937.

further reading: *The Railways of*

Pembrokeshire. Pub. H.G. Walters.

TRECYNON HALT

Opened on 1 May 1911 with up and down platforms between Aberdare (High Level) and Hirwain.

TREFERIG JUNCTION

Unadvertised stopping place on the Taff Vale Railway between Beddau Colliery and Glyn Colliery. In use by miners from 1892 until about September 1928.

TREFOREST ESTATE HALT

Island platform serving a large industrial estate between Taff Wells and Treforest Low Level. It is believed the original intention was

Trawsfynyyd Camp and which was located near to the station of the same name.

Trawsfynydd Lake Halt and depicted in the summer of 1949.

L.G.R.P. 19224

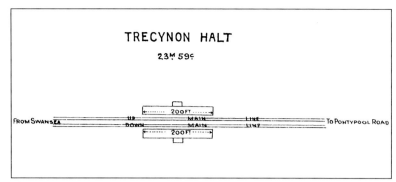

Trecynon Halt, depicted on 24 May 1958.

GWT / M. Hale

to call this 'Trading Estate Halt.' Opening date not reported and although 1942 is quoted, the location does not appear in Bradshaw for that year. However, on 26 January 1948 authorisation was given for expenditure of £520 on lavatory accommodation although the final figure quoted was less at £475.

TREFOREST HALT

On the Cardiff Railway between Treforest Low Level (Taff Vale Railway) and Rhydefelin Halt. Up and down platforms were to have been provided although the stopping place was never in fact opened because of a lengthy legal battle which precluded the opening of this part of the Cardiff Railway line.

TREHOWELL HALT

Opened on Saturday 27 July 1935 with up and down platforms and located between Weston Rhyn and Chirk. Authorisation had been given

Busy times at the unadvertised Tremain's Halt on 3 June 1942 and with workers to leave from the down platform around 3.30 p.m.

National Railway Museum / GWR B 'Box' 378/24

85

on 28 March 1935 and with the cost stated to be £269 for 80ft.' x 8ft. platforms, footpaths, steps to road, shelters, name and notice boards, fencing, gates, lighting and drainage.

TRELEWIS HALT

Authorised on 26 April 1934 with up and down platforms 200ft. long, shelters, booking office, paths to road and name and notice boards. Estimated cost of £307. Opened 9 July 1934 and situated between Nelson and Treharris. On 3 October 1935 booking office and waiting room accommodation was authorised for an estimated £160.

an illustration appears on page 24 of, *Steam in South Wales Vol 6*. Pub. Welsh Railway Record Circle.

TRELEWIS PLATFORM

Up and down platforms situated between Nelson & Llancaiach and Taff Merthyr Colliry Halt. Opened on Monday 9 July 1911.

an illustration appears on page 17 of, *Steam in South Wales Vol 5*. Pub. Welsh Railway Record Circle.

TREMAIN'S FACTORY HALT

Island platform fronting up and down loops on the South Wales Main line between Bridgend and Pencoed. In use sometime after 1928 and renamed 'Tremain's Platform' by 1941.

TREMAINS PLATFORM

see entry for Tremains Factory Halt.

TRENCH HALT

On the Cambrian system between Overton-on-Dee and Elson Halt. Single platform which first appeared in the timetable in December 1914. Closed from 10 June 1940 and reopened 6 May 1946.

Trewerry & Trerice on the single line south of Newquay and pictured in 1922.   *L.G.R.P. 8837*

TREOWEN HALT

Staggered up and down platforms either side of a road over bridge, and situated between Pentwyn-mawr and Crumlin High Level. Access was via a set of steps from a nearby bridge and a pagoda shelter was provided on at least one of the platforms. Opened on 14 March 1927.

TRERHYNGYLL & MAENDY HALT

Situated between Cowbridge and Ystradowen. Single platform with corrugated pagoda - the building being unusual in that there were a large pair of corrugated doors in one end. Opened on 1 May 1905, although apparently raised to station status by 1922. Indeed, Taff Vale timetables never used the term Platform for this place in their timetables or tickets despite the fact that no shelter was provided until after the grouping. Other platforms on this line and which had opened at the same time did have the suffix throughout their working lives.

further reading: *The Cowbridge Branch*. Pub. OPC.

TREWERRY & TRERICE HALT

Opened on 14 August 1905, single platform on the Truro and Newquay line south of Newquay.

further reading: *The Newquay Branch*. Pub. OPC.

TRIMSAREN JUNCTION

Miners' stopping place between Pinged Halt and Trimsaren Road. In use between 1909 and 1927.

TRIMSAREN ROAD PLATFORM

Single masonry platform with public access from a path leading down from an over bridge. Opened 2 August 1909. Located between Kidwelly Branch Junction and Glyn Abbey Halt and raised to station status sometime between 1910 and 1922.

TROEDYRHIWFUWCH COLLIERY HALT

Staggered up and down platforms in use by 1901 between Tir Phil and Troedyrhiwfuwch Halt.

THOEDYRHIWFUWCH HALT

Up and down platforms between Pontlottyn Colliery Halt and Tip Phil. Opened 1 April 1908, and closed 1 January 1916.

TROEDYRHIW HALT

Opened 18 February 1907 on the joint GWR / Rhymney Railway route from Quakers Yard to Merthyr. Located between

GREAT WESTERN RAILWAY.

GENERAL MANAGER'S OFFICE,

Circular No. 2712.   PADDINGTON, W.2.

G. 2655.   25th March, 1920.

BRENTFORD BRANCH.

The Rail Motor Service between Southall and Brentford will be restored as from Monday, April 12th, and BRENTFORD Station and TRUMPER'S CROSSING Halt will be re-opened for passenger traffic.

Particulars of the train service will be issued by the Superintendent of the Line.

CHAS. ALDINGTON,

General Manager.

TRUMPERS CROSSING HALT

1 M.   39 c.

151 FT.

UP BRANCH LINE

FROM BRENTFORD   BRENTFORD BRANCH   To SOUTHALL

DOWN BRANCH LINE

151 FT.

Complete with temporary appendages to blend in with the coach, '517' 0-4-2T No. 833 pauses at Trumpers Crossing Halte. Two members of the class had at this time the temporary panelling seen. This was fitted around 1906/7 but had been removed by 1911. Others of the class though carried a pseudo coach livery until around 1924.

Real Photographs 51214

Abercanaid and Aberfan. On 4 November 1910 authorisation was given for an extension of both platforms by (or to ?) 250ft. Waiting rooms provided on both platforms with access from a bridge carrying the public road across the railway. Note - Passenger services ceased from 12 February 1951, but it is thought that this halt remained open for unadvertised colliery trains until 1 November 1954. The line was singled when regular passenger services ceased. Which would accord with the reduction to one platform. There is no timetable evidence for Clinker's assertion that the original name had no suffix - Bradshaw for 1910 uses 'Halt' and for July 1922 'Platform'. From 1924 the term Halt appears to have been used.

TRUMPER'S CROSSING HALT

Located between Southall and Brentford. Up and down platforms opened 2 May 1904 as 'Trumpers Crossing Halte' although originally intended to have been called, ' Trumpers Crossing for Osterley Park'. (Early photographs show the name Trumpers Crossing for Osterley Park Halte.)Temporary closure from 22 March 1915 to 12 April 1920. Permanent closure from 1 February 1926.

TRUTHALL BRIDGE HALT

see entry for Truthall Halt.

TRUTHALL HALT

Single platform able to accommodate just one coach between Nancegollan and Helston authorised on 8 June 1904, and opened on 1 July 1905. Although officially designated as a 'Platform' in July 1906, the designation 'Halt' was restored at an unreported time. Tickets however referred to Truthall Bridge Halt.

further reading: *The Helston Branch Railway*. Pub. Oakwood Press.

TUTSHILL HALT (FOR BEACHEY)

Located within a deep cutting between Chepstow and Wye Valley Junction. Up and down platforms 150ft long with shelters, and accessed via a long descending stairway. Opened on Monday 9 July 1934. A booking office was located at road level. Authorisation by the GWR had been on 26 April 1934 with the originally intended name of 'Wye Valley Junction Halt'. The estimated cost was £525.

an illustration appears in, *Steam in South Wales Vol 4.* Pub. OPC.

TWYFORD ABBEY HALT

Located between Brentham and Park Royal West. Provided with up and down platforms with shelters. Opened on 1 May 1904 and closed on 1 May 1911 following a landslip and which had badly damaged the facilities. See also entry for Brentham Halt which was built as substitute for Twyford Abbey Halt using some salvaged materials including the pagoda shelters. (It may have been that the up platform did survive for some time and continued to be served by rail-motors.)

Truthall Halt recorded in 1920 and at the time just 15 years old. At a later stage the length of the platform here was reduced considerably and in its final years could accommodate just a single coach.

L.G.R.P. 8397

TYCOCH

Situated between Trimsaren Road and Kidwelly and unadvertised. 'Halt' suffix not believed to have been carried although it did appear on tickets whilst 'Tycoch Platform' appeared in the working time-tables. Facilities consisted a single platform facing a siding off the branch. Dates of use are confusing with some references to closure by 19 September 1927, and others concerning an opening on this date,

a ticket though was issued from the location in October 1945.

TYDDYN BRIDGE HALT

Opened 1 December 1930. Single platform between Frongoch and Capel Celyn Halt.

TY-FYSTON HALT

Single platform at the site of what was later Biglis Junction neat Cadoxton. Reported as opened by

An undated, but nevertheless pre 1914 view of Trumpers Crossing Halte. The name of the location was apparently taken from a local landowner, although it was also reported that he had been somewhat un-coperative in connection with the provision of the facilities here.

National Railway Museum 334/87

January 1888 and closed by October 1888. Although reference is made to the 'Halt' suffix in plans the use of the word must be open to question for the period.

TYGWYN HALT

Between Talsarnau and Harlech. Single timber platform 71ft. long with flat roofed corrugated shelter opened 11 July 1927. In 1943 it was reported that an average of 311 passengers used the stopping place daily. Similar figures were reported for Talwrn Bach Halt.

further reading: *The Cambrian Coast Railway.* Pub. Foxline.

TYLACOCH PLATFORM

Staggered up and down platforms between Treorchy and Treherbert. Opening date not reported but possibly 5 June 1905 when Gyfeillon Platform was opened elsewhere on this line. Closed in November 1912.

TYLER'S ARMS PLATFORM

see entry also for Bournville Halt (Monmouth). An agreement dated 20 April 1916 between the GWR and John Lancaster & Co. relates to the construction of Tylers Arms Colliers Platform. Facilities referred to include up and down platforms 400ft. x 9ft. with a shelter on the up side.

TYLLWYN HALT

Located between Victoria and Ebbw Vale Low Level. Facilities consisted a long masonry built single platform fronting the single passenger line, a goods line and several sidings. Surmounting this was a small flat roof brick shelter open at the front. The stopping place opened on 26 November 1943.

TYLWCH HALT

Between Llandiloes and Pantydwr

on the Moat Lane to Three Cocks Junction line. Formerly a station it was downgraded from 10 July 1939.

TYNYCWM HALT

Located between Risca and Rogerstone. Authorised on 13 December 1934 at an estimated cost of £1,590. Island platform provided 250ft x 14ft. together with veranda covering, footbridge to public road, booking office, w/c, name and notice boards. Opened on 17 April 1935. On either 20 January 1937 or the same date in 1938, authorisation was given for an extension of the footbridge for an estimated £307, so as to give access to the stopping place from the down side of the line.

TYR CELYN PLATFORM

see entry for Tir Celyn Platform.

Above: Upper Soudley Halt and with the original facilitates of a platform just 14 inches above rail level. This was replaced in 1908 and after the stopping place had been in existence only about one year.

National Railway Museum / GWR

Right: The Forest railmotor service at the Halt, circa 1910. A point of interest is that the spelling of the word Halt had already been corrupted into the English version at this early stage.   *Collec. Ian Pope.*

UNDY HALT

Situated between Severn Tunnel Junction and Magor. Authorised on 29 June 1933 with timber up and down platforms 150ft. x 9ft., shelters, name and notice boards, fencing and lighting. Estimated cost of £278. In addition the lamp hut formerly at Sebastapol Halt was refixed at the site for an additional £4 becoming the booking office. Opened on 11 September 1933, the shelters provided here were of brick, having a sloping corrugated roof and open at the front. Access was by means of a footbridge from the nearby road which served each platform.

UP-EXE HALT

Originally a station reduction to 'Halt' status occurred from 1 October 1923. Facilities consisted of a single platform located between Burn Halt and Thorverton. Supervision exercised from Thorverton.

further reading: *The Exe Valley Railway*. Pub. Kingfisher.

UPPER AND LOWER PENN HALT
see entry for Penn Halt

UPPER BOAT HALT

On the Alexander, (Newport and South Wales) Docks & Railway system between Dynea Halt and Groeswen Halt. 'Halt' suffix given from 1 July 1924 to avoid confusion with Upper Boat on the former Cardiff Railway. Up and down rail level platforms provided.

UPPER LYDBROOK

Situated on the joint GWR / Midland system between Drybrook Road and Lower Lydbrook. Formerly a public station used for excursion traffic from 8 July 1927 to 27 June 1937. Up and down platforms existed although it is not clear if both were used by the excursion traffic.

further reading: *The Severn & Wye Railway Vol. 3*. Pub. Wild Swan.

UPPER SOUDLEY HALT

Single 146ft. platform with shelter opened on 3 August 1907, and located between Newnham and Cinderford.

further reading: *The Forest of Dean Branch Vol. 1*. Pub. Wild Swan.

UPTON-BY-CHESTER HALT

On the Chester to Birkenhead railway between Chester and Mollington. Opened on 17 July 1939, the opening having been deferred for an unknown reason from 4 July 1938. Up and down platforms provided.

UPTON LOVEL CROSSING

Unadvertised stopping place between Heytesbury and Codford and used by workmen, probably in connection with military activities around 1915. (Possible spelling may also have been ...LOVELL...)

UPWEY WISHING WELL HALT

Located between Dorchester and Upwey Junction. Up and down timber platforms 150ft. long provided with shelters and opened 28 May 1905. The location was popular for many years with visitors to the nearby Wishing Well.

further reading: *The Story of the Westbury to Weymouth Line*. Pub. OPC.

*Upper Soudley in 1961, and one of Ben Ashworth's superbly atmospheric photographs from the Forest of Dean.
The locomotive, 57xx, No. 7788 still displays 'GWR' on the tank side and has paused briefly at the remains of
the Halt and officially for a 'blow-up', although co-incidentally the 'White Horse' was situated just out of sight
along the road. The break has also allowed an unofficial visitor the chance of a glimpse at the footplate, whilst
the whole scene including the road sign just breaths nostalgia.*

B.J. Ashworth

*Probably recorded not long after opening, Upwey Wishing Well Halte, and with a Dorchester / Yeovil bound
steam-railmotor in the platform.*

Lens of Sutton

Great Western Railway Halts

— V —

VICARAGE CROSSING HALT

Situated between Coed Poeth and Berwig Halt. Single wooden platform with corrugated iron shelter opened 1 May 1905. Temporary closure from 1 January 1917 to 2 April 1917, and permanently closed from 1 January 1931. Access was from a by-road from the Ruthin Road and protected by a level crossing, controlled by a gate keeper.

Great Western Railway Halts

— W —

WAINFELIN HALT

Authorised on 14 December 1911 and situated between Pontypool Crane Street and Cwmffrwdoer Halt. Opened 13 July 1912 with facilities consisting up and down platforms 150ft. x 9ft., shelters 20ft. x 7ft., steps and pathway. The estimated cost of the facilities is given as £526. Temporary closure reported from 30 April 1917 although sometime after this the facilities were dismantled. On 6 October 1927 authorisation was given for a new halt at the same location and with the same equipment as previously. The estimated cost on this occasion was £689. A note in the records states, "...the original halt had been dismantled...". Re-opening occurred on 30 April 1928. (It is likely some items must have remained at the site after 1917 as otherwise, especially allowing for inflation, the rebuilding cost would surely have been greater.) Closed 5 May 1941.

WAINHILL CROSSING HALT

Opened on 1 August 1925 and located between Bledlow Bridge and Chinnor. Single low height platform provided with access from an adjacent level crossing. It is not believed any public shelter was provided and neither was the 'Halt' suffix displayed. Receipts included with Watlington.

further reading: *Country Branch line Vol 2*. Pub. Wild Swan.

WALFORD HALT

Single platform located between Ross-on-Wye and Kerne Bridge. Opened on 23 February 1931 with 120ft. platform. The staff from neighbouring Kerne Bridge were responsible for the upkeep of the location.

further reading: *The Ross, Monmouth and Pontypool Road Line*. Pub. Oakwood Press.

WARREN HALT

Opened on 1 July 1905 * and located between Dawlish and Starcross. Originally provided with short up and down platforms these were lengthened in 1906 at a cost of £299. 0s 9d. By 1907 the name 'Warren Platform' was displayed. Renamed 'Dawlish Warren' from 1 October 1911. Closed on 23 September 1912. (On 24 November 1910 authorisation was given for a station to replace the Halt on a new site 17 chains north. This was opened on 23 September 1912 and consisted of up and down platforms fronting up and down running loops.) * Although the July opening date is given, authorisation for construction had not been given until as late as 28 June and it is likely then that the opening may have been on 1 August. 1 July had been the date for the commencement of the railmotor services in the area, and it may well have been that the July date was given simply to keep matters 'tidy'.

Further reading - a very comprehensive record of the location is in, *Exeter - Newton Abbot: A Railway History*. Pub. Platform 5.

The crossing keeper at Wainhill Crossing Halt attending to the gates after the departure of a train towards Watlington on 29 June 1957.

Hugh Davies

Walford Halt viewed towards Kerne Bridge. As can be gathered from the view, the line at this point was on a gradient of 1 in 100 and which favoured trains from Ross-on-Wye. *Lens of Sutton*

Warren Halt / Platform and with a Teignmouth bound steam railmotor in the platform. Again there is a variation on the type of shelter used, the design of those nearest the camera believed unique to the location.
Great Western Trust

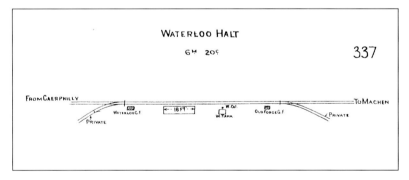

WARREN PLATFORM

see entry for Warren Halt.

WARWICK CAPE YARD

see entry for Royal Agricultural Show ground Warwick.

WATERLOO HALT

On the Caerphilly branch between Machen and Gwernydomen Halt and served by trains in the down direction only. (The up and down lines are split at this point so only a single platform was necessary. The corresponding Halt for down traffic was known as Fountain Bridge Halt.) First appeared in the timetable in October 1908 with very basic facilities consisting of a single 18ft. platform, lamp and nameboard. Unlike the other halts on these lines, the suffix did not appear on the nameboard.

WATERLOO ROAD BRIDGE HALT

1911 proposal for a stopping place between Oakengates and Wellington - not proceeded with.

WATTSTOWN PLATFORM

Situated between Ynyshir and Pontygwaith Platform. Up and down platforms opened on 5 June 1905 and closed on 12 July 1920.

WEADE SIDING

Unadvertised stopping place between Defiance Halt and Wiveliscombe used by workmen between 1905 and November 1915 in connection with the construction of the deviation line.

WELFORD PARK

Stopping place on the Lambourn Valley line between Boxford and Great Shefford. Originally provided with a single low-height platform, under Great Western control from 1905, a passing loop was installed together with standard-height platforms and pagoda shelters. The new facilities were 150ft. long and a ticket office was situated off the end of the up platform. Although designated a Halt by the GWR the no suffix was displayed whilst goods and parcels traffic were handled.

further reading: *The Lambourn Branch*. Pub. Wild Swan.

WELSH HOOK HALT

Situated between Mathry Road and Wolf's Castle Halt. No suffix displayed but the name board proclaimed 'for St. Lawrence'. Round-topped corrugated iron shelter on one side and small sloping timber shelter on the other side. Rail level platforms opened 5 May 1924.

further reading: *The Railways of Pembrokeshire*. Pub. H.G. Waters.

WELSHPOOL SEVEN STARS

Stopping place serving the narrow gauge Welshpool and Llanfair Railway between Welshpool and Raven Square. Closed 9 February 1931.

WERN HIR HALT

Single platform provided between Usk and East Access Halt. Unadvertised, so dates of use are not reported although given its location it is very likely that it was used in connection with Glascoed ROF Factory.

WEST ACCESS HALT

see entry for Glascoed Factory West Access Halt.

WESTBURY-ON-SEVERN HALT

Opened on 9 July 1928 and provided with up and down platforms 126ft. x 8ft. with shelters, footpaths, steps and gates. Located between Grange Court and Newnham. Estimated cost of construction put at £435.

WEST EALING ENGINERING DEPOT

Situated between West Ealing and Hanwell & Elthorne. Used by railway workmen from about 1907 to November 1915.

WEST EXE HALT

Located between Tiverton and Cadeleigh. Single platform provided with timber shelter which opened either 9 or 19 March 1928. Estimated cost of £172. On 29 April 1937 authorisation was given for an extension of the platform together with improved lighting at an estimated cost of £110, although the final amount was £160.

Welford Park on the Lambourn Valley Branch. This was the only passing loop on what was otherwise 12 miles of single line from the junction at Newbury. L.G.R.P. 8419

On a very wet day an unidentified 57xx heads west past the ground level facilities at Welsh Hook Halt on a Carmarthen to Fishguard working.
Andrew Muckley

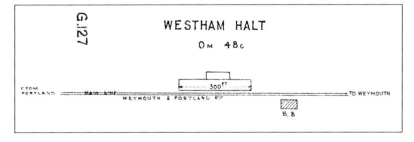

further reading: *The Exe Valley Railway*. Pub. Kingfisher.

WESTHAM HALT

Single 300ft platform with shelter authorised on 20 May 1909 and situated between Melcombe Regis and Rodwell. Opened on 1 July 1909 with access from nearby Littlefield level crossing. The platform was reported as having been lengthened in February 1913.

further reading: *The Isle of Portland Railways*. Vol. 2. Pub. Oakwood Press.

WESTON MILTON HALT

Between Worle Junction and Weston-Super-Mare. Authorised

West Exe Halt looking towards Tiverton. This was by far the busiest of the minor stopping places on the Exe Valley line and in consequence the extension seen was provided in 1937. Most patronage being from shoppers travelling to Exeter.

Lens of Sutton

Westbury-on-Severn Halt viewed in the 'up' direction - towards Gloucester, in 1950.

Real Photographs 22946

4161 at Weston-Under-Penyard Halt with the 4.00 p.m. Gloucester to Hereford service on 7 August 1964.

B.J. Ashworth

on 23 March 1933 with up and down platforms 250ft. x 8ft., shelters, footpaths and steps. Estimated cost of £843. Opened on 3 July 1933. On 30 May 1946 electric lighting was authorised in place of paraffin vapour at an estimated cost of £300. Receipts were reasonable from the outset and showed a steady climb from £101 in the first full year of operation, 1934, to £213 by 1938. This latter figure corresponded to a reported 2,308 ticket sales together with 32 seasons.

WESTON-SUPER-MARE EXCURSION PLATFORM.

Located on a spur from Weston Milton and in use by July 1897. Became a public station (Weston-Super-Mare Locking Road) after July 1924.

WESTON-UNDER-PENYARD HALT

Opened 2 December 1929. Single platform provided between Ross-on-Wye and Mitcheldean Road.

WEST RHONDDA HALT

see entry for Celtic Halt.

WESTWOOD HALT

see Stretton Westwood Halt / Stretton Westwood Crossing Halt.

WHIMSEY HALT

Located between Bilson Junction and Drybrook Halt. Single 150ft. platform with shelter. Opened 3 August 1907 with parcels and 'miscellaneous' traffic handled until 1 March 1914. Remained open for passengers only, but closed from 7 July 1930.

WHITCHURCH DOWN PLATFORM

351ft. single platform provided between Tavistock and Horrabridge. Opened on 1 September 1906 with a waiting room and booking office from which parcels traffic was handled.

Whitchurch Down Platform on the Plymouth to Launceston line. This was one of five locations on the GWR to have the name Whitchurch, two of which were classified as halts.

Lens of Sutton

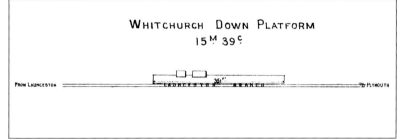

Whitehall Halt on the Culm Valley line from Tiverton Junction. The siding to the left held just three wagons and dated from independent Culm Valley Railway days. Its value though must surely be questionable. A practice typical of the branch was for newspapers to be left by the Guard of passing trains within the waiting shelter and which would then be collected by the local residents.

further reading: *The Tavistock, Launceston & Princetown Railways*. Pub. Oakwood Press.

WHITCHURCH HALT

Between Pensford and Brislington. Single 150ft. solid concrete platform with corrugated pagoda opened on 1 January 1925. The estimated cost of the stopping place was put at £320 although that actually recorded was £358. 12s 6d.

further reading: *Through Country-side and Coalfield*. Pub. OPC.

White Hart Halt on the Caerphilly Branch and opened by the GWR in May 1947. The variation in levels between the up and down lines is also apparent from the photograph.

L.G.R.P. 26210

Willersley Halt seen looking south towards Honeybourne. Slightly unusual here was the fact that on the up platform the shelter was partly on the platform, whilst on the opposite side it stood wholly to the rear.

Lens of Sutton

WHITEBROOK HALT

Single standard height platform with timber front, but filled in at the rear and with a round-topped corrugated iron shelter. Located between St. Briavels and Penallt Halt, and opened 1 February 1927.

WHITE CITY

On the joint GWR / Metropolitan Railway system between Latimer Road and Shepherds Bush. Formerly a public station which opened in May 1908, was closed on 1 November 1914, and was thereafter used for excursion traffic

under the name of 'Wood Lane'. Up and down platforms provided.

WHITEHALL HALT

Single platform between Culmstock and Hemyock. Opened 27 February 1933.

further reading: *The Culm Valley Railway.* Pub. Twelveheads Press,

WHITE HART HALT

On the Caerphilly branch between Machen and Fountain Bridge Halt / Waterloo Halt. Opened on 12 May 1947 with separate up and down platforms on opposite sides of the main Newport to Caerphilly road and consequently at considerably differing levels. Both platforms were at rail level and consisted only of a single sleeper edge, a nameboard and a lamp. There was also a board crossing.

WHITE HOUSE HALT

Proposal for a halt on the ill-fated and never built line from Wolverhampton to Bridgnorth.

further reading: *The Railway to Wombourn.* Pub. Uralia Press.

WHITEHURST HALT

See entry for Llangollen Road Halt and also Appendix 1.

WHITLOCK'S END HALT

Located between Shirley and Grimes Hill & Wythall. Authorised on 24 March 1936 at an estimated cost of £819. Up and down platforms provided and which were opened on 6 July 1936.

WHITWORTH HALT

see entry for Corrwyg Merthyr Navigation Colliery Halt and also Mercantile Colliery.

WILLERSEY HALT

Between Weston-Sub-Edge and Broadway. Up and down platforms 100ft. long were opened 1 August 1904. Sometime after November

1906 the platforms were extended to 152ft. at a cost of £30.

further reading: *The Stratford on Avon and Cheltenham Railway.* Pub. Irwell Press.

WINDMILL END HALT

Up and down platforms provided between Dudley and Old Hill. Formerly a station and downgraded at an unreported date and with the suffix added in the timetable from 15 September 1952.

WINDSOR COLLIERY HALT

Single platform between Abertridwr and Senghenydd.

WINGFIELD VILLAS HALT

Between Plymouth (North Road) and Devonport (Albert Road). Up and down platforms provided. Opened 1 June 1904, and closed in June 1921.

WISTANSTOW HALT

Opened 7 May 1934 between Craven Arms & Stokesay and Marsh Farm Junction. Up and down platforms provided.

WIVELISCOMBE

Unadvertised stopping place situated between Wearde siding and St. Germans Viaduct. Used by workmen in conjunction with work on the new deviation line between 1905 and November 1915.

WNION HALT

Opened 5 June 1933. Single platform between Bontnewydd and Drws-y-nant.

WOLF'S CASTLE HALT

Situated between Welsh Hook Halt and Clarbeston Road. Authorised on 1 May 1913 with 120ft. standard-height platforms, shelters, footpath and steps at an estimated cost of £373. Opened 1 October 1913 with varying length platforms, - up side 115ft. and down side 155ft., each accessible by a series of steps leading down from a nearby road over-bridge.

Timber shelters provided of unusual design having a sloping valance at the front, and closed on three sides. Goods and parcels traffic handled, with the name board proclaiming, '...for Treffcarne Rocks.'

further reading: *The Railways of Pembrokeshire.* Pub. H.G. Waters.

WOLLERTON HALT

Authorised on 30 July 1931 at an estimated cost of £270, and opened on 2 November 1931. Staggered up and down platforms provided between Tern Hill and Hodnet.

WOLVERCOT PLATFORM

Situated between Oxford and Yarnton. Authorised on 30 October 1907 with up and down platforms at an estimated cost of £521. Opened 1 February 1908, and closed in January 1916. (Another stopping place, Wolvercote Halt was located on the nearby LNWR line. This closed in 1924.)

The shelter at Windmill End Halt, certainly non standard and portraying its former station status.

National Railway Museum / B.R. 'C' Series 13196

Left:

The joint GWR / LMS Wistanstow Halt and 18 miles 31 chains south of Shrewsbury not far from the junction for the Bishop's Castle Railway.
Lens of Sutton

Centre left:

Almost at the opposite end of the system from the above view was that at Wolf's Castle Halt, and between Clarbeston Road and Letterston Junction. The additional lettering read, 'for Trefcarne Rocks'.
Philip J. Kelley.

Facing page:

BR Standard Class 4, No. 75023 on a Ruabon to Barmouth train at Wnion Halt on 31 August 1964.
Andrew Muckley

The only view so far located of Wolvercot Platform north of Oxford and sometimes incorrectly referred to as a Halt. According to Stanley Jenkins the location had originally been staffed and was administered by a lady in this post during the World War One.
Lens of Sutton.

Wood Lane Exhibition Station on the electrified GWR / Metropolitan Railway. Despite officially designated a Halt the former glory of the location is readily apparent.

Wootton Rivers Halt on the Berks and Hants Extension line and probably recorded soon after opening. Interestingly and despite the presence of the churns, official records refer only to passenger traffic being handled here and which peaked in 1930 with £227 of revenue for the issue of 2,865 tickets together with seven season tickets. From 1934 onwards a signal box was also provided, located just off the west end of the up platform, and which principal use was to increase line occupancy on what was the main route to the west.

The approach to Wootton Rivers Halt and with details of the local agent who would issue tickets. Such provision was common at numerous halts and platforms.

WOOD END PLATFORM

Up and down platforms 400ft. long with shelters situated between The Lakes Halt and Danzey. Opened 1 July 1908 with parcels traffic also handled. The suffix was dropped from 7 July 1924.

WOOD LANE

see entry for White City.

WOODVILLE ROAD HALT

see entry for Cathays (Woodville Road) Platform.

WOOTTON RIVERS HALT

Between Savernake (Low Level) and Pewsey. Up and down platforms originally 200ft. long provided at an estimated cost of £740 and with 12ft. x 8ft. round topped shelters and an oil hut also provided. Opened 24 September 1928.

WOOTTON WAWEN PLATFORM

Opened 1 July 1908 with 370ft. up and down platforms with shelters. Located between Alcester Branch Junction and Henley-in-Arden. Receipts included with the latter station.

WORTHY DOWN PLATFORM

Between Sutton Scotney and Kings Worthy. Single 450ft. platform on the east side of the line and used by the Royal Flying Corps to serve a nearby air station from 1 April 1918. Became a public stopping place from 1921 with receipts included with Kings Worthy. In the winter of 1942/3 the facilities were rebuilt to include a new island platform and brick shelter. (Renamed Worthy Down Halt in 1951.)

further reading: *The Didcot, Newbury & Southampton Railway.* Pub. Wild Swan.

WYESHAM HALT

Situated between Monmouth and Redbrook-on-Wye. Authorised on 30 October 1930 with an open

6904 'Charfield Hall' passing Wootton Wawen Platform with, according to the headcode, a Class 'A' working. The engine was one of batch of the class dating from 1940 and would survive in service until 1965.

Real Photographs K3426

Worthy Down Halt, as it was then, recorded circa 1955. The location served a large military camp out of view to the left and was frequented principally by service personnel.

Lens of Sutton

Wyesham Halt, and recorded by J. Dagley-Morris on 3 January 1959.

framed single timber platform with round-topped corrugated iron shelter at an estimated cost of £202. Opened 12 January 1931.

WYKE REGIS HALT

Authorised on 20 May 1909 for a 300ft. single platform estimated to cost £443. Opened 1 July 1909 and located between Sandsfoot Castle Halt and Portland. On 17 March 1910, additional access to the stopping place from the east side was authorised for an estimated £21.

further reading: *The Isle of Portland Railways. Vol. 2.* Pub. Oakwood Press.

WYNDHAM HALT

Opened 10 August 1942. Single platform between Ogmore Vale and Nantymoel.

WYNN HALL HALT

Located between Plas-y-Wern junction and Pant Halt. Single platform opened 1 May 1905, and closed and dismantled 22 March 1915.

WYNNVILLE HALT

Up and down platforms located between Ruabon and Johnston & Hafod. Opened 1 February 1934.

WYRE HALT

Authorised on 23 March 1924 with up and down platforms 150ft. x 8ft. and located between Pershore and Fladbury. Estimated cost of the facilities £476. Opened 11 June 1934.

WYTHALL

See entry for Grimes Hill Platform.

Left: Wyre Halt viewed towards Worcester on a wet late October day in 1965. The lamps are of the GWR 'Challow' type and fuelled by paraffin vapour. This meant they had to be charged at regular intervals, hence the windlass visible at the foot of the posts. The name 'Challow' was taken from the station at which the type had first been used.

Andrew Muckley

Below: Wyke Regis Halt on the joint Portland Branch - hence the approach of the LSWR engine. In later years an additional shelter was added to the platform and which itself was also rebuilt in stone. A private siding also led to Whitehead's Torpedo Factory behind the photographer.

YARDLEY WOOD PLATFORM

400ft. up and down platforms with shelters reported as first used from 1 July 1908. Suffix dropped from 7 July 1924. Facilities were considerable for a 'Platform', and consisted of brick buildings, long platforms and staff. Access between the platforms was via an over-bridge. Located between Hall Green and Shirley.

YEALMPTON

On the branch from Plymstock. Formerly a public station which closed on 7 July 1930. In use by workmen from 21 July 1941 until re-opened as a public stopping place from 3 November 1941. Finally closed from 6 October 1947.

further reading: *The Yealmpton Branch*. Pub. OPC.

YEO MILL HALT

Between East Anstey and Bishops Nympton & Molland. Single platform opened 27 June 1932.

YEOVENEY HALT

see entry for Runnemeade Range.

YNYSYBWL HALT

see entry for Ynysybwl (New Road) Platform.

YNYSYBWL (NEW ROAD) PLATFORM

On the Taff Vale system between Robertstown Halt and Clydach Court Loop Junction. Single platform opened 1 November 1904 with the suffix dropped prior to 1922. Re designated Halt status from 7 May 1945.

Above: Yardley Wood Platform and not as stated on the post card 'Station', although it is just possible to discern the correct designation from the additional word on the running-in board.

Lens of Sutton

Above: The former Yealmpton Station and which was downgraded to 'Halt' status after re-opening in 1941. It is seen here prior to first closure in 1930 and at which time was still classified as a station.

Below: Yeo Mill Halt on the Banstaple Branch from Taunton. The Halt was on the north side of the single line and with Exmoor in the background.

Yeoveney Halt, and the third and final name for the same location on the Staines Branch from West Drayton.

Ticketing Arrangements at Halts and Platforms

- by Stephen Berry

The subject of the ticketing arrangements for the various Platforms and Halts is understandably involved and no universal "fit-all" account can be given. In the first instance, it is probably easiest to deal with those places which had a booking office or at least a member of staff in attendance to issue tickets.

Most of these issued the traditional Edmonson card ticket either from stock stored in the usual rack (e.g. Undy Halt) or from a clip board (e.g. Caldicot Halt). It was common, but by no means universal, for the GWR to include in small type on the ticket the name of the supervising station. However, a word of caution is necessary, in that not all Edmonson tickets including the small-type name were actually issued at the halt concerned - some were held in the booking office at the supervising station itself. For short journeys it seems as though paper excess tickets were made out at the destination station. A further variation applied to some lines which were open only for non-public workmen's services and where a week's worth of tickets would be sold in one lot. This system applied on the colliers' service from Aberdare to Nantmelyn, for instance.

On a number of routes, particularly but not exclusively those where rail motors or auto trains provided the passenger service, the guard also acted as the conductor, issuing "ladder" tickets showing the name of each stopping place and using a bell punch machine to indicate the required destination. A stock of tickets of different prices was held on a clipboard and thus one particular type of ticket could be used for several different journeys. Examples of services using this type of ticket are the Chalford - Gloucester route and the lines converging on Monmouth. They were, however, also used on such routes as the Cambrian Coast line and the Aberystwyth to Carmarthen line, both of which had large numbers of unstaffed halts. However, on certain routes (e.g. Old Hill to Dudley and the Ynysybwl branch) thin card tickets were issued for specific journeys, though some of these had multiple choice points of origin or destination.

So far then the issuing methods mentioned have been traditional - i.e. by railway staff from booking offices or on the train. However, certain favoured locations had far from traditional arrangements in the form of a local agent and who sold tickets on a commission basis from premises convenient to the halt. Though no complete list of locations covered in this way can be given, those halts known to have had this facility are Cross Hands, Dilton Marsh, Farrington Gurney, Gresford, New Passage, Wootton Rivers and Wyre.

Though many halts would have had only paper tickets for public consumption, it is thought that most if not all would have had card stocks of privilege tickets held at their supervising station. Until the early 1960s any railwayman wanting to book a privilege ticket had to do so by firstly completing a request form, which was handed to the booking clerk with the cash in exchange for the ticket. Certainly the tiny Carreghofa Halt, which, as far as is known dealt with public bookings by passengers paying at their destination and receiving a paper excess ticket, had privilege single and privilege return blank card tickets held in the booking office at Llanymynech.

It will be seen then that a variety of possibilities existed - indeed, there may have been other schemes not covered by these notes. However, the statistics seem to show that the GWR did by-and-large manage to collect most of the fares due and undoubtedly any losses which did exist were relatively small, bearing in mind that most journeys would have been local. Those halts which did hold stocks of tickets generally held those for only a small selection of local destinations, though exceptions to this rule would be stocks of the more popular excursion and "cheap" destinations. The exception to the rule came with those few halts which served large forces barracks. These halts certainly held the traditional local stocks but also had quite an amazing variety of printed Forces Leave tickets. For instance, Tinkers Green Halt, serving the large army depots just outside Oswestry, had printed Forces Leave Return tickets to such wide-ranging destinations as Edinburgh, Glasgow, Leeds, Sheffield, Colchester and Bristol.

Though it would take a separate volume to deal with this subject in depth, it is hoped that these few notes will be of interest in showing that building and opening a halt could be a simple matter compared with subsequent arrangements for its administration!

Above, below, and facing page: Avoncliffe Halt and which basic facilities survived little altered from 1906. The track spacing increases through the platform due to the presence of the Kennet and Avon Canal aqueduct that passes over the railway behind the photographer.

All: A. Attewell

Appendix 1

New information, additions and addendum to Volume 1 of

'Great Western Halts'

Page 2 - Photograph of Chalford railmotor shed. This burnt down in January 1916 also destroying railmotor No. 48.

ABBEY FOREGATE PLATFORM. (SHREWSBURY) - So described in Bradshaw for April 1910. Previously a ticket platform serving the down line only. Then used as an alighting point. Closed 30 September 1912.

ABERBRAN HALT - On the Brecon to Neath line between Cradoc and Devynock & Sennybridge. Previously a station which was reduced in status from 5 May 1941.

ABERDARE COMMERCIAL STREET PLATFORM - see Commercial Street Platform

ABERDYLAIS - Opened 24 September 1851with stone built platforms each having a timber building. Unstaffed and renamed 7 June 1954.

ABERERCH HALT - Between Penychain and Pwllheli. It was a request stop, certainly up to the summer of 1922, though trains had scheduled stops by September 1924. It was unstaffed and renamed from 1 May 1956.

ABINGDON ROAD HALT - Typographical error, closure date should read 22 March 1915 only.

ADMASTON - Opened 1 June 1849 as a station, downgraded and renamed 30 June 1952.

ALL STRETTON HALT - Temporarily closed from 4 January 1943 to 6 May 1946.

ALVERLEY HALT - It is thought that the colliery opened in 1939 and that the halt opened about the same time. Never appeared in public timetables.

ARDDLEEN - Became Arddleen Halt in public timetables from 14 June 1954. Until the grouping, trains stopped only on Mondays and Wednesdays. Thereafter a daily service was provided.

ASHTON GATE PLATFORM - Opening date should read 15 September 1906 for football supporters only. Public opening from 1 October 1906. Timber platforms provided. Temporary closure from 1917 (probably January when several other economies were introduced on the branch) to 23 May 1926 at which time it re-opened with masonry platforms.

ASTWOOD HALT - Reported as closed, 'owing to the suspension of the diesel car service.'

AYNHO PARK PLATFORM - The suffix was certainly used in the timetables until September 1924, it was dropped by July 1935 and reinstated during the early 1950's.

BALA LAKE HALT - Closed 25 September 1939.

BEACHLEY JUNCTION - Unadvertised stopping place between Woolaston and Chepstow. Believed only a platform on the down side, and used by workmen between 18 November 1918 and 3 March 1919.

BEAUFORT - This was the end of the line, but no platform was ever provided.

BILSON HALT - Closed 1 November 1920.

BLACK DOG HALT - Further reading: *The Calne Branch*. Pub. Wild Swan.

BLACK LION CROSSING HALT - Opened to public services on 1 January 1906 and closed on 22 September 1924. Remained open for unadvertised colliery trains until c.1932.

BLAENCORRWG HALT - See entry for North Rhondda Halt.

BRENTHAM HALT - Reported as closed from February 1915 for duration of the war. Re-opening date 29 March 1920. Suffix not used in timetables after reopening, however tickets show, 'Brentham Platform'.

BRITISH RHONDDA HALT - See also entry for Pontwalby Halt. This halt was served by a railmotor service from Swansea East Dock which terminated here and then departed from the same platform by means of a crossover. It was never served by through trains in either direction.

BULLO CROSS HALT - See entry also for Ruddle Road Halt.

CAPE HALT - Opened before 1912.

CAPEL CELWYN HALT - Typographical error, name should read CAPEL CELYN and situated between Frongoch and Arenig.

CASSINGTON HALT. - Typographical error, location should read Eynsham.

CEFN COED - On the Merthyr to Pontsticill line. A passing place with two platforms and substantial buildings but unstaffed from 1 March 1934. Reduction in status was never reflected in the public timetable although the working timetable contained the footnote, 'Cefn Coed and Pontsarn are worked as Halts.' See also entry for Pontsarn.

CEFN COED COLLIERY HALT - Situated between Cilfrew and Crynant on the Neath to Brecon line. Opened 8 September 1930 and consisting of a single short platform with a shelter, nameboard and lamp.

CHELTENHAM HIGH STREET HALT - Authorised on 18 March 1908 with up and down platforms, shelters, steps, subway and gates. Estimated cost of £1248. (Concrete pagoda shelters were provided - see information under Newbury West Fields Halt.)

CHURCH VILLAGE HALT - It seems this was originally a staffed station, and reduction in status together with addition of Halt suffix occurred on 14 March 1932. The status as a 'Halt' did not appear in the public timetable.

COMBE HAY HALT - For cost of construction see also entry for Radford & Timsbury Halt.

Above and facing page: Detail of Carradoc Falls Halt and recorded during 1960/1.   *All: A. Attewell.*

COMMECIAL STREET PLATFORM - Between Aberdare (TVR) station and Mill Street Platform. Opened 26 December 1904 and closed in June 1912.

CORRWYG MERTHYR NAVIGATION COLLIERY HALT - Platform length was 118feet.

CRADOC HALT - Between Brecon and Aberbran on the Brecon to Neath line. Formerly a station it was downgraded on 1 December 1945, although never in the public timetable.

CRAIGLONG BRIDGE HALT - Typographical error, name should read Craiglon Bridge Halt.

CRAY HALT - Between Devynock and Craig-y-Nos on the Brecon to Neath line. Formerly a station, downgrading occurred on 1 June 1942, although never in the timetables.

CROSS HANDS HALT - See also New Passage and Pilning Halts.

CWMNOEL HALT - Typographical error, should read Cwmneol Halt.

CWMSFYIOG HALT - Suffix appeared on the nameboard, but not in timetables or on tickets.

DOLSERAU HALT - Typographical error in appendage. This should read, 'for Torrent Walk.'

DOLYGAER HALT - Originally opened as a station in 1863. Suffix not carried on the nameboard although it did appear on the tickets. Unstaffed from 21 March 1932.

DRYBROOK HALT - There was a pit between the rails allowing loco crews to rake out the fire during stop-overs. The photographs of the stopping place on P.77 (Volume 1) were taken prior to November 1908 when the original 1foot 2inches high platforms used at the halts in the Forest of Dean were raised to standard height.

DUFFRYN CROSSING HALT - Typographical error. Date of authorisation should read February 1914.

DYNEA HALT - delete last sentence.

DYNES HALT - Delete reference.

EARDINGTON - According to Clinker, date of downgrading was 1 April 1949.

ELLERDINE HALT - Typographical error. Should read "between Crudgington and Peplow."

EVAILVACH HALT - More probably Efail Fach, which was the spelling used in the Board of Trade Inspector's report of 5 February 1921 when it was

reported that a single 80 feet long platform had been provided. Situated between Maesmelyn Colliery Halt and Tonmawr Halt, it was opened in 1920 and used until at least 1924.

FENNANT ROAD HALT - Closed 22 March 1915.

FFRONFRAITH HALT - Opened between August 1922 and September 1924.

FFONGOGH - It must be doubted whether this was ever considered a Halt, as it offered the full range of facilities for passengers and goods until closure and was also in charge of a substantive station-master.

GANANT HALT - This was opened in 1908 and was in fact the branch platform for trains on the Gwaun-cau-Gurwen service. The 'Halt', a brick built single platform, was just to the rear of the station platform and connected to it by a short path - in effect it created a 'V' station, although since the branch was worked by rail motors the distinction may have been preserved for booking purposes. Closure took place on 4 May 1926 - hence 'Not in use at present' in 1928. See also page P.94 of Volume 1, Gors-y-Garnant.)

GELLIRHAID CROSSING - possibly situated at grid reference SS999878 and where a lane from Gellirhaid Farm crosses the Hendre Forgan - Ely Valley Line; or at Gellirhaid Junction, Grid Ref. ST007872,

GLANRHYD HALT - Originally a station opened in 1858 but closed to passengers on 20 July 1931. Re-opened as Glanrhyd Halt on 21 December 1938.

GLARN-YR-AFON HALT - Typographical error, should read Glan-yr-Afon Halt. Further reading: *The Mid Wales Railway*. Pub. Oakwood.

GLYNTAFF HALT - Opened 1 September 1904.

GOITRE HALT - Opened between August 1922 and September 1924.

GOLANT HALT - Opened 16 September 1895. Temporary closure in 1917 as shown. Further temporary closures from 1 January 1940 to 9 February 1942, 24 August 1942 to 3 October 1942 and 2 May 1944 to 2 October 1944.

GOTHERINGTON HALT - Between Bishop's Cleeve and Gretton Halt on the Cheltenham to Honeybourne line. A former station, it was downgraded on 1 January 1941 although not in the timetables.

GREAT SOMERFORD HALT - Further reading: *THE MALMESBURY BRANCH*. Pub. Wild Swan.

GRIMES HILL & WYTHALL PLATFORM - A very good view of this stopping place complete with a miniature pagoda, possibly in use as a toilet, appears in *The Great Western in the West Midlands*. Pub. OPC.

GROESWEN HALT - Opened 1 September 1904. Platforms were at rail level.

GWAELODWAEN COLLIERY - Correct name is Gwaelodywaen Colliery.

GWERNYDOMEN HALT - Rail level facilities consisting of a simple lamp and nameboard.

GYFEILLON PLATFORM - Opened 5 June 1905, closed July 1918.

HAFODYRYNYS PLATFORM - The building to which the suggestion refers was not that shown, but the main building on the other platform, which was similar in style to that at Aynho Park Platform (see page 23 Vol. 1). This building was demolished before closure. Suffix did not appear on nameboards, but did on tickets and timetables.

HAUGHTON HALT - Facilities should read staggered 'up' and 'down' platforms.

HEATH HALT (Cardiff Railway) - Staggered platforms were provided at the time of opening.

HIRWAUN POND HALT - Opened 23 July 1941. Situated on the Pontypool Road - Neath line between Hirwaun and Rhigos Halt and opened to serve the eastern part of the ROF factory which. After the Second World War, became a trading estate.

HIRWAUN TRADING ESTATE - This was situated within the factory / estate and was served by a branch which left the Pontypool Road - Neath line between Hirwaun and Hirwaun Pond. It may well have opened at the same time as Hirwaun Pond Halt, but no record of the actual date has been traced.

HOTWELLS HALT - Was also known as Hotwells Extension Platform.

KELMSCOTT & LANGFORD - Although the status is unclear, it remained staffed throughout its existence, though only partially for the final three years. It also handled goods, livestock and parcels traffic.

LEGACY - Situated between Rhostyllen and Rhos, both of which opened to passenger traffic on 1 October 1901. However it would seem that Legacy opened 1 March 1905 with the introduction of railmotor services on this line and its branch to Ponkey Crossing, as it is not shown as handling passenger or parcels traffic in the 1904 RCH Handbook. Contrary to this view is the fact that the local press, writing about the opening to passengers in 1901, mentions Legacy as a 'stopping place merely' - i.e. not a station. It had a brick platform 304 feet long and small brick building and a goods yard. It was never given the suffix in timetables and remained open for parcels after closure to passengers on 1 January 1931.

LEWISTOWN HALT - Location should read, between Blackmill and Ogmore Vale.

LIGHTMOOR PLATFORM - Opened 12 August 1907 on or near the site of Lightmoor Station which was open for traffic between 1 October 1855 and 1 November 1864. Closure had caused some local resentment and this had periodically resulted in appeals to the GWR for a reopening.

LITTLE DRAYTON HALT - Closed 6 October 1941.

LITTLE STRETTON HALT - Temporarily closed from 4 January 1943 to 6 May 1946.

LLANBRADACH COLLIERY HALT - Location should read on the Caerphilly to Rhymney line just north of Llanbradach Station.

LLANDARCEY PLATFORM - Closure date of 4 October 1947.

LLANDAVEY HALT - Possibly this entry was a typographical error in the original source material with the information pertaining to Llandarcy Halt.

LLANDOUGH PLATFORM -Rail level platforms. Closed 1 June 1918.

LLANFAREDD HALT - Further reading: *The Mid Wales Railway*. Pub. Oakwood.

LLANFECHAIN HALT - On the Llanfyllin branch. Formerly a station, it was downgraded from 1 April 1940.

LLANGOLLEN ROAD HALT - Renamed 'Whitehurst Halt' by 1910 and 'Whitehurst Platform' in 1935. Then 'Whitehurst' in 1947.

LLANGORSE LAKE HALT - Further reading: *The Mid Wales Railway*. Pub. Oakwood.

LLANGYBI - Opened in 1869, at first on market and fair days only. By 1904 it was handling parcels and horse boxes and by 1910 it was in daily use. It is likely that it became staffed at this time, but it became unstaffed again on 28 November 1947.

LLANSTEPHAN HALT - Further reading: *The Mid Wales Railway*. Pub. Oakwood.

LLANSTEPHEN CROSSING - Opened in 1925 for the Royal Welsh Agricultural show and situated between Carmarthan Junction and Sarnau on the line to Fishguard. Closed on 8 August 1925 when the show finished.

LLANGOLLEN ROAD HALT - Shelters provided on both platforms together with a lamp hut and booking hut on the up side.

LODGE HALT - Opened in 1905 and closed 1 January 1931.

LONG SUTTON & PITNEY. - Described in Bradshaw as a 'Halt' in April 1910 although not by 1922.

LOWER LODES HALT - Typographical error by the GWR! The villages are actually spelt 'Loders'.

LOWER SOUDLEY - The platform here was used by Dulcote Leatherboard Co. who had a works at the nearby Camp Mill.

LYDSTEP PLATFORM - Reopened 8 July 1935.

Another of Austin Attewell's wonderful detail views, this time of Cwmffrwd Halt on the Blaenavon Branch. Halts and Platforms are rarely seen modelled and yet the basic simplicity of such a location would afford for a wonderful accurate representation without excessive effort.

Appendix 2

Post Nationalisation passenger closure dates.

Aberbran Halt	15-10-1962	Cadoxton Terrace Halt	15-10-1962
Abercamlais Halt	15-10-1962	Capel Celyn Halt	4-1-1960
Abercwmboi Halt	2-4-1956	Caradog Falls Halt	14-12-1964
Aberdylais	15-6-1964	Carreghofa Halt	18-1-1965
Abertafol Halt	14-5-1984	Cashes Green Halt	2-11-1964
Admaston	7-9-1964	Cassington Halt	18-6-1962
Alberta Place Halt	6-5-1968	Cattistock Halt	3-10-1966
Alford Halt	10-9-1962	Cefn Coed	13-11-1961
All Stretton Halt	9-6-1958	Cefn Coed Colliery Halt	15-10-1962
Alltddu Halt	22-2-1965	Cefn On Halt	21-9-1986
Alphington Halt	9-6-1958	Celynen North Halt	30-4-1962
Alverley Colliery Halt	9-9-1963	Celynen South Halt	30-4-1962
Ammanford Colliery Halt	18-8-1958	Chedworth	11-11-1961
Arddleen	18-1-1965	Chiseldon Camp Halt	11-11-1961
Ashton Gate Platform	7-9-1964	Chittening Platform	23-11-1964
Aynho Park Platform	7-1-1963	Christian Malford Halt	4-1-1965
		Chudleigh Knighton Halt	9-6-1958
Backney Halt	12-2-1962	Church Village Halt	31-3-1952
Baptist End Halt	15-6-1964	Churn Halt	10-9-1962
Bargoed Colliery Halt	31-12-1962	Ciliau Aeron Halt	12-9-1951
Bathford Halt	4-1-1965	Clearbrook Halt	31-12-1962
Beanacre Halt	7-2-1955	Cloy Halt	10-9-1962
Beaufort	2-10-1961	Clydach Court Halt	28-7-1952
Beavers Hill Halt	15-6-1964	Clyne Halt	15-6-1964
Beddau Halt	31-3-1952	Coed Ely	9-6-1958
Bedlinog Colliery Junction	After June 1954,	Coldharbour Halt	9-9-1963
	not later than 15-6-1964	Collingbourne Kingston Halt	11-11-1961
Berwyn	14-12-1964	Commins Coch Halt	14-6-1965
Bittaford Platform	2-3-1959	Coole Pilot Halt	9-6-1963
Black Dog Halt	20-9-1965	Copper Pit Platform	11-6-1956
Black Rock Halt	13-8-1976	Coryates Halt	1-12-1952
Blaenplwyf Halt	12-2-1951	Cound Halt	9-9-1963
Blaisdin Halt	2-11-1964	Cove Halt	7-10-1963
Bledlow Bridge Halt	1-7-1957	Coxbank Halt	9-9-1963
Bolham Halt	7-10-1963	CradocHalt	15-10-1962
Bonwm Halt	14-12-1964	Craiglon Bridge Halt	21-9-1953
Boughton Halt	5-4-1965	Cray	15-10-1962
Bourneville Halt	30-4-1962	Creech St.Michael Halt	5-10-1964
Bowbridge Crossing Halt	2-11-1964	Cross Hands Halt	23-11-1964
Box (Mill Lane) Halt	4-1-1965	Crossways Halt	12-2-1951
Boxford	4-1-1960	Crumlin Valley Colliery Platform	6-11-1961
Bradford Peverell & Stratton Halt	3-10-1966	Crynant New Colliery Halt	After 1954
Brampford Speke Halt	7-10-1963	Culmstock	9-9-1963
Brean Road Halt	2-5-1955	Cutnall Green Halt	5-4-1965
Brimley Halt	2-3-1959	Cwmavon (Mon) Halt	30-4-1962
Brimscombe Bridge Halt	2-11-1964	Cwmbach Halt	15-6-1964
Brockweir Halt	5-1-1959	Cwmffrwd Halt	30-4-1962
Bromham & Rowde Halt	18-4-1966	Cwm Prysor Halt	4-1-1960
Broughton Gifford Halt	7-2-1955	Cwmsyfiog Halt	31-12-1962
Bryncelynog Halt	4-1-1960	Cwmsyfiog Colliery Halt	31-12-1962
Bryngwyn Halt	18-1-1965	Cymmer Corrwg	1955
Bullo Cross Halt	3-11-1958	(unadvertised from 22-9-1930)	
Burlish Halt	5-1-1970	Cynonville Halt	2-1-1956
Burn Halt	7-10-1963		
Burrator Halt	5-3-1956	Darby End Halt	15-6-1964

Dillwyn & Brynteg Halt	15-10-1962		Ham Green Halt	7-9-1964
Dolsarau Halt	29-10-1951		Ham Mill Crossing Halt	2-11-1964
Dolygaer Halt	31-12-1962		Haughton Halt	12-9-1960
Donyatt Halt	10-9-1962		Hawkmoor Halt	
Dorton Halt	7-1-1963		Became Pullabrook Halt (qv)	13-6-1955
Doseley Halt	23-7-1962		Hayles Abbey Halt	7-3-1960
Downfield Crossing Halt	2-11-1964		Hendford Halt	15-6-1964
Duffryn Rhondda Halt	6-3-1967		Hightown Halt	10-9-1962
(unadvertised from 3-12-1962)			Hoelgerrig Halt	13-11-1961
Dunsford Halt	9-6-1958		Hirwaun Pond Halt	15-6-1954
Dynes Halt	17-9-1963		Hirwaun Trading Estate	By 9-1953
			Horspath Halt	7-1-1963
East Access Halt	By 6-1954		Hunnington	1-9-1958
Eastbury	4-1-1960			
East Garston	4-1-1960		Ide	9-6-1958
Easthope Halt	31-12-1951		Ilmer Halt	7-1-1963
Ebley Crossing Halt	2-11-1964		Ilton Halt	10-9-1962
Ellerdine Halt	9-9-1963		Ingra Tor Halt	5-3-1956
Elliot Pit Colliery Platform	31-12-1962			
Elms Bridge Halt	30-5-1955		Jackament's Bridge Halt	17-9-1948
Elson Halt	10-9-1962		Jackfield Halt	
			(1st. - replaced by new halt)	1-3-1954
Farley Halt	23-7-1962		Jordanston Halt	6-4-1964
Farringdon Gurney Halt	2-11-1959			
Felindyffryn Halt	14-12-1964		Kelmscott & Langford	18-6-1962
Felin Fran Halt	11-6-1956		Ketley Town Halt	23-7-1962
Fleur-de-Lis Platform	31-12-1962		Kidwelly Flats Halt	11-11-1957
Forge Crossing Halt	5-2-1951		Kingston Crossing Halt	1-7-1957
Fountain Bridge Halt	17-9-1956		King Tor Halt	5-3-1956
Four Oaks Halt	13-7-1959			
			Lacock Halt	18-4-1966
Gadlys Bridge Platform	2-4-1949		Lando Platform	15-6-1964
Garneddwen Halt	18-1-1965		Laverton Halt	7-3-1960
Glan Llyn Halt			Ledbury Town Halt	13-7-1959
(formerley Flag Station Halt,			Lewistown Halt	4-6-1951
renamed 25-9-1950)	18-1-1965		Lewknor Bridge Halt	1-7-1957
Glan-yr-Afon Halt	31-12-1962		Liddaton Halt	31-12-1962
Glascoed Crossing Halt	After 1954		Lightmoor Platform	23-7-1962
Glasgoed Halt	13-10-1957		Little Stretton Halt	9-6-1958
(unadvertised from 30-5-1955)			Llafar Halt	4-1-1960
Glascoed ROF	24-4-1961		Llanbradach Colliery	By June 1954
Glyn Abbey Halt	21-9-1953		Llandogo Halt	5-1-1959
Glyncorrwg	2-11-1964		Llandow Halt	15-6-1964
(unadvertised from 22-9-1930)			Llandow (Wick Road) Halt	15-6-1964
Gogarth Halt	14-5-1984		Llanerch-Ayron Halt	12-2-1951
Golant Halt	4-1-1965		Llanfaredd Halt	31-12-1962
Goonbell Halt	4-2-1963		Llanfechain Halt	18-1-1965
Goonhavern Halt	4-2-1963		Llangorse Lake Halt	31-12-1962
Gotherington Halt	13-6-1955		Llangower Halt	18-1-1965
Great Shefford	4-1-1960		Llangybi	22-2-1965
Green Bank Halt	23-7-1962		Llanstephen Halt	31-12-1962
Greenway Halt	13-7-1959		Llys Halt	18-1-1965
Gretton Halt	7-3-1960		Longdon Halt	9-9-1963
Groesfaen Colliery Platform	31-12-1962		Lower Penarth Halt	14-6-1954
Groesffordd Halt	31-12-1962		Lydstep Halt	2-1-1956
Groswen Halt	17-9-1956		Lyng Halt	15-6-1954
Gwaelodywaen Colliery	By 6-1954			
Gwernydomen Halt	17-9-1956		Maindy Halt	15-9-1958
			Malswick Halt	13-7-1959
Hafodyrynys Platform	15-6-1964		Manningford Halt	18-4-1966
Halberton Halt	5-10-1964		Margam Halt	2-11-1964
Halesowen	1-9-1958		Marine Colliery Halt	2-10-1961

Marston Halt	7-2-1955	Pontcynon Bridge Halt	16-3-1964
Marteg Halt	31-12-1962	Pontgwaith Halt	12-2-1951
Mary Tavy & Blackdown Halt	31-12-1962	Pontrhydyrun Halt	30-4-1962
Matthewstown Halt	16-3-1964	Pontsarn Halt	13-11-1961
Melyncourt Halt	15-6-1964	Pontyberem	21-9-1953
Milton Halt	4-6-1951	Pontwalby Halt	15-6-1964
Mitchell & Newlyn Halt	4-2-1963	Pontypool (Blaendare Road) Halt	30-4-1962
Mithian Halt	4-2-1963	Poyle Halt	29-3-1965
Monks Risborough	15-1-1986	Probus & Lacock Platform	2-12-1957
(replaced by new station)		Pullabrook Halt	
Monkton & Came Halt	7-1-1957	(formerly Clearbrook Halt)	2-3-1959
Morebath Junction Halt	3-10-1966		
Mount Hawke Halt	4-2-1963	Radipole Halt	2-1-1984
		Raglan Road Crossing	30-5-1955
Nantewlaeth Siding Halt	1955	Rhigos Halt	5-6-1964
Nantgarw Halt (High Level)	17-9-1956	Rhosmedre Halt	2-3-1959
Nantmelyn Platform	2-4-1949	Rhydyfelin Halt (High Level)	2-2-1953
Nantyffyn	After 1954	Robertstown Halt	28-7-1952
Neath Engine Shed	After 1954	Rodmarton Platform	6-4-1964
Netherhope Halt	5-1-1969	Rollright Halt	4-1-1951
Newbury West Fields Halt	4-2-1957	Rowton Halt	9-9-1963
New Dale Halt	23-7-1962	Rushwick Halt	5-4-1965
Newland Halt	5-4-1965	Ruspidge Halt	3-11-1958
New Passage Halt	23-11-1964		
North Filton Platform	23-11-1964	St. Harmons	31-12-1962
North Rhondda Halt	3-1963	St.Mary's Crossing Halt	2-11-1964
Northwood Halt	9-9-1963	Saltney	12-9-1960
Nottage Halt	9-9-1963	Sampford Peverell Halt	5-10-1964
		Sandsfoot Castle Halt	3-3-1952
Oaksey Halt	2-11-1964	Sarsden Halt	3-12-1962
Ogilvie Colliery Platform	31-12-1962	Scafell	
Ogilvie Village Halt	31-12-1962		7-3-1955
Old Hill Halt	15-6-1964	Sebastapol	30-4-1962
Oldwoods Halt	12-9-1960	Semington Halt	18-4-1966
Old Ynsybwl Halt	28-7-1952	Sesswick Halt	10-9-1962
Oldmarch Halt	22-2-1965	Shaugh Bridge Platform	31-12-1962
		Shipton-on-Cherwell Halt	1-3-1954
Pans Lane Halt	18-4-1966	Silian Halt	12-2-1951
Pantsgallog Halt High Level	2-5-1960	Slough Depot	15-1-1956
Pantyffordd Halt	15-10-1962	Six Bells Halt	30-4-1962
Pantywaun Halt	31-12-1962	Snatchwood Halt	5-10-1953
Parcyrhun Halt	13-6-1955	South Aylesbury Halt	5-6-1957
Park Hall Halt	7-11-1966	South Marston Factory Platform	30-6-1957
Pebworth Halt	3-1-1966	South Pit Halt	2-11-1964
Pedair Ffordd	15-1-1951	Speen	
Pembrey Halt	21-9-1953		4-1-1960
Penallt Halt	5-1-1959	Stanley Bridge Halt	20-9-1965
Pencarreg Halt	22-2-1965	Stanner	5-2-1951
Penpont Halt	15-10-1962	Stanwardine Halt	12-9-1960
Penscynor Halt	15-10-1962	Staple Edge Halt	3-11-1958
Pentrecourt Platform	15-9-1952	Staverton Halt	18-4-1966
Pentrefelin	15-1-1951	Stockcross & Bagnor	4-1-1960
Pentrefelin (Glam) Halt	11-6-1956	Stoke Prior Halt	15-9-1952
Pentremawr Colliery Siding	21-9-1953	Strap Lane Halt	5-6-1950
Pentwynmawr Halt	15-6-1964	Stratford-on Avon Racecourse Platform	
Penydarren Platform	After 6-1954		25-3-1968
Perranporth Beach Halt	4-2-1963	Stratton Park Halt	7-12-1964
Pilning Low Level	23-11-1964	Sun Bank Halt	5-6-1950
Pinewood Halt	10-9-1962	Swanbridge Halt	6-5-1968
Pinged Halt	21-9-1963		
Plas-y-Court Halt	12-9-1960	Taff Merthyr Colliery Halt	15-6-1964
Plym Bridge Halt	31-12-1962	Talsarn Halt	12-2-1951

Teigl Halt	4-1-1960		
Teigngrace	2-3-1959	Wainhill Crossing Halt	1-7-1957
The Hawthorns Halt	29-4-1964	Walford Halt	5-1-1959
Thorney & Kingsbury Halt	15-6-1964	Waterloo Halt	17-9-1956
Tinkers Green Halt	18-1-1965	Welford Park	4-1-1960
Tintern Quarry Siding	After 6-1954	Welsh Hook Halt	6-4-1964
Tir Celyn Halt	After 1950	Wern Hir Halt	30-5-1955
Tonteg Halt (Cadoxton Line)	10-9-1962	Westbury-on-Severn Halt	10-8-1959
Tonteg Halt (Llantrisant Line)	31-3-1952	West Exe Halt	7-10-1963
Towersey Halt	7-1-1963	Weston-Under-Penyard Halt	2-11-1964
Trawsfynydd Lake Halt	4-1-1960	Westham Halt	3-3-1952
Trecwn Sidings	3-8-1964	Westwood Halt	31-12-1951
Trecynon Halt	15-6-1954	Whitchurch Down Platform	31-12-1962
Treforest Halt	17-9-1956	Whitchurch Halt	2-11-1959
Trehowell Halt	29-10-1951	Whitebrook Halt	5-1-1959
Trelewis Halt	15-6-1964	Whitehall Halt	9-9-1963
Trelewis Platform	15-6-1954	White Hart Halt	30-6-1952
Tremains Factory Halt	2-11-1964	Whitehurst Halt	12-9-1960
Trench Halt	10-9-1962	Willersey Halt	7-3-1960
Treowen Halt	11-7-1960	Windmill End Halt	15-6-1964
Trehyngyll and Maendy Halt	26-11-1954	Wistanstow Halt	11-6-1956
Trewerry & Trerice Halt	4-2-1963	Wnion Halt	18-1-1965
Troedyrhiw Halt	12-2-1951	Wolf's Castle Halt	6-4-1964
Truthall Platform	5-11-1960	Wollerton Halt	9-9-1963
Tutshill Halt	5-1-1959	Woodville Road Halt	15-9-1958
Tycoch Halt	By 5-1949	Wootton Rivers Halt	18-4-1966
Tyddyn Bridge Halt	4-1-1960	Worthy Down Halt	7-3-1960
Tyllwyn Halt	30-4-1962	Wyesham Halt	5-1-1959
Tylwch Halt	31-12-1962	Wyke Regis Halt	3-3-1952
Tynycwm Halt	30-4-1962	Wyndham Halt	5-5-1958
		Wynnville Halt	12-9-1960
Undy Halt	2-11-1964	Wyre Halt	3-1-1966
Up Exe Halt	7-10-1963		
Upper Boat Halt	17-9-1956		
Upper Soudley Halt	3-11-1958		
Upwey Wishing Well Halt	7-1-1957		

Note: Closure dates for locations not listed are also mentioned in the text if this occurred prior to 1948 or are not known.

Suburban DMU set at Foley Park between Kidderminster and Bewdley on a through working from Birmingham Snow Hill in March 1958. This location is typical of where recent records are more difficult to trace than those of years previous and no formal closure date is given. It is likely to have been around the same time as Northwood Halt near Bewdley, in 1963. Unlike the latter location though this stopping place was totally demolished after closure and has not seen a resurrection under Severn Valley Railway ownership. Anthony A. Vickers

Appendix 3

Halts opened by British Railways.

CEFN TILLA HALT

Between Llandenny and Usk. Opened 4 June 1954, closed 30 May 1955.

CHESTERTON LANE HALT

Between Kemble and Cirencester Town. Opened 2 February 1959, closed 6 April 1964.

CHURCH'S HILL HALT

Between Kemble and Culkerton. Opened 2 February 1959, closed 6 April 1964.

COLNBROOK ESTATE HALT

Between West Drayton and Colnbrook. Opened 1 May 1951, closed 29 March 1965.

HADNOCK HALT

Between Symonds Yat and Monmouth (May Hill).

Opened 7 May 1951, closed 5 January 1959.

JACKFIELD HALT

Between Coalport and Ironbridge. Opened 1 March 1954, closed 9 September 1963.

PARK LEAZE HALT

Between Kemble and Cirencester Town. Opened 4 January 1960, closed 6 April 1964.

SOUTH MARSDEN FACTORY PLATFORM

Unadvertised platform at the end of a short branch off the Highworth Branch from Stratton. Re-opened 27 December 1956.

TROUBLE HOUSE HALT

Between Culkerton and Tetbury. Opened 2 February 1959, closed 6 April 1964.

Opposite and above, B.R.'s attempt at pursuing the Halt principals during the 1950's were both varied in approach and also with regards to success. At a time when branch and secondary routes were experiencing major inroads into revenue it was perhaps questionable that locations were suggested for such wayside stopping places where there had never been a demand before - Trouble House Halt on the Tetbury branch, and illustrated on the opposite page, a clear example. In other locations though the railway was slow to respond to suburban housing development and could perhaps have achieved welcome revenue if respond times had been equal to road operators. In any event those new stopping places that were build were often in the austere concrete of the period, as indeed was used to rebuilt numerous existing stopping places. The scene above being Poyle Estate Halt on the Staines Branch and looking towards West Drayton.   *Both: Andrew Muckley*

Llandogo Halt.

J. Dagley-Morris

Appendix 4

Known Ticket Platforms on the GWR.

	First Reported Use	Date of Closure
Abbey Foregate (Shrewsbury)	June 1887	30 September 1912
Bodmin	October 1897	July 1902
Chester	1886	May 1905
Churston	October 1897	July 1902
Dolgelly	1886	
Falmouth		1 May 1903
Gwinear Road		1 January 1903
Heathfield	October 1897	July 1902
Helston		1 January 1903
Kingswear	July 1897	November 1915
Minsterley	July 1902	January 1905
Mortonhampstead	October 1897	July 1902
New Milford	July 1897	January 1905
Newquay	October 1897	July 1902
Penzance	July 1897	January 1905
St. Erth	July 1897	1 January 1903
St. Ives	July 1897	1 January 1903
Swansea Eastern Depot		
Truro		1 May 1897

Evening at Walford Halt.   *J. Dagley-Morris*

SR.25103

Ministry of Transport
Berkeley Square House
London, W.1.

9 December 1946

Sir,

I have the honour to report for the information of the Minister of Transport that, in accordance with the Appointment of 13 December 1937, I made an inspection on 26 November 1946, of the new Halt at Pebworth on the Honeybourne-Stratford on Avon line of the Great Western Railway. I was accompanied by Brigadier C.A. Langley.

This halt consists of Up and Down timber trestle platforms each 150ft. Long and 8ft. In width; shelters are provided on both platforms with one lamp about in the middle of each platform. Access to platforms on both sides is provided by steps and ramps leading from a public road which crosses the line by an underbridge adjacent to the halt.

There is an appreciable passenger user, 876 passengers having entrained during September 1946, in addition to 114 Season Ticket holders. The normal daily service consists of 13 rail motors and 4 trains. In the case of the latter the guard collects tickets and sees that passengers are in the right portion of the train for the platform; no difficulty has been experienced in this respect.

The works are complete and in good order, and, subject to the provision of additional facilities which may become necessary in the event of a substantial increase in usage I recommend that they be approved.

I have the honour to be, Sir,
Your Obedient Servant,

The Secretary   (Sgd.)   A.C. Trench
Ministry of Transport   Colonel